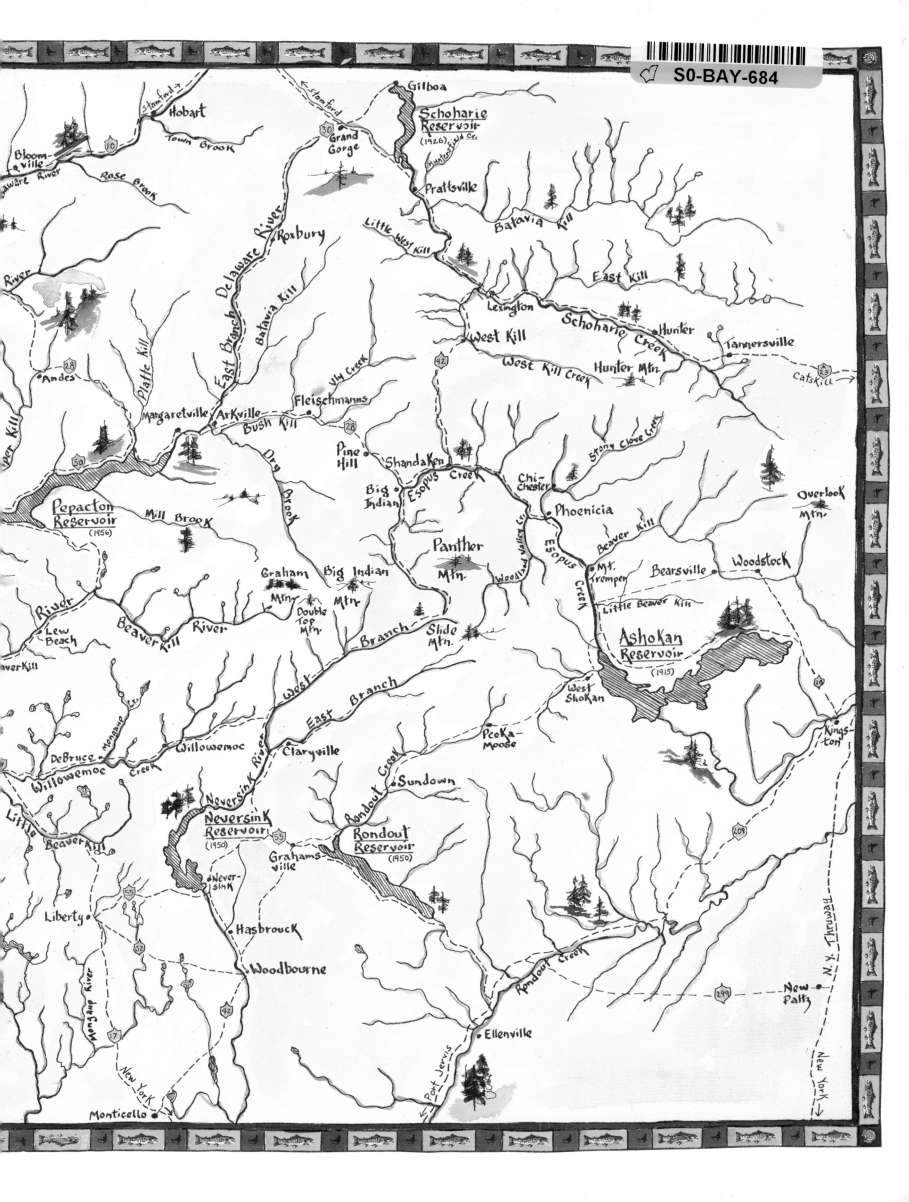

Land of Little Rivers

Canterbury Creek, **Asher B. Durand, oil on canvas, 1846.**
The Catskills are a well-watered mountainland compounded of Cooper's tales and the Psalms of David, deep forests and green peaks, no lava flows, no vast sterilities of sand or ice. The holy of holies, however, has always been a quiet place. Let sublimity stun. The heart warms easier to serenely sloping ranges and the sweet-scented streams of man's oldest pursuit.—T. MORRIS LONGSTRETH

Private collection, photograph courtesy Vose Galleries of Boston.

A Catskill Gallery

~~~~~~~~~~~~~~~~~~~~~~~~~~~~~~~~~~

I zaak Walton's influence, said Patrick Chalmers, "has made almost every poet a bit of a fisherman and, beyond a doubt, every fisher-man a bit of a poet." Beautiful trout streams like those of the Catskills will do that to you; they have done exactly that not only to poets but also to countless painters, photographers, writers, and others of creative bent. We are fortunate that some of the best of these have been influenced by our mountains and little rivers, including the painters Worthington Whittredge, Asher B. Durand, Thomas Doughty, and writers like John Burroughs and T. Morris Longstreth.

The mass of the southern Catskills rises in ranged domes, which on that morning dropped into gulfs made pearl-gray by the mists of melting snow. Westward the chain that walls the valley toward Lexington wandered away until it grew soft with lilacs and lavenders.
—T. MORRIS LONGSTRETH

Lower Beaverkill River.

Photograph by Kris Lee.

Long Eddy, Delaware River.

When the Indians chose Mountains of the Sky as the name for the refuge of Manitou, they did not mean the high sky, the empty and interminable blue. They meant the low, rich, all-brooding heaven that settles in between the ranges with its wash of gentian shades. They meant the cloud-heaps of pearl or ivory that west winds set adrift from their moorings in these mountains.
—T. MORRIS LONGSTRETH

Dry Brook.
The bed of the stream has been scooped out of the solid rock. Here and there banks of sand have been deposited, and accumulations of loose stone disguise the real nature of the channel . . . there are other places where everything has been swept clean; nothing remains but the primitive strata, and the flowing water merrily tickles the bare ribs of mother earth. There are long, straight, sloping troughs through which the water runs like a mill-race . . . as if someone were pouring it very steadily out of a pitcher, and from which it glides away without a ripple, flowing over a smooth pavement of rock which shelves down from the shallow foot to the deep head of the pool.—HENRY VAN DYKE*

Fly Fishing, **Worthington Whittredge, oil on canvas, 1866.**

But the prettiest thing was the stream soliloquizing in such musical tones there amid the moss-covered rocks and boulders. How clean it looked, what purity! An ideal trout brook was this, now hurrying, now loitering, now deepening around a great boulder, now gliding evenly over a pavement of green-gray stone and pebbles; no sediment or stain of any kind, but white and sparkling as snow-water, and nearly as cool. —JOHN BURROUGHS

Peekamoose Gorge, Rondout Creek.
Then steal up the little gorge and sit at the foot of the thread of water that falls into the quiet bowl. The shrunken stream only whispers now, but in the stillness you can think back to the time when you heard it roaring. It seems now more likable, if less splendid. And the woods are thinking it all over. Leaves fall one by one, and here and there shafts of light shine down where the woods were lately dark. If you sit quite still you may see a thrush drink from the pool or hear the chirp of some passing bird. A red squirrel is busy on the upper bank, and the bell of the distant train tells you that there were once people here. Otherwise you have only the Falls and the weight of endless time.
—T. MORRIS LONGSTRETH

Little Falls,
Beaverkill River.

Enrico's Zen Quartet.
Along the Beaverkill where I have fished for thirty-six years, there is a different wildflower show each week during the trout season. The trout fisherman who is unaware of this is missing half the fun.
—VICTOR T. NORTON

Below Kellam's Bridge, Delaware River.

**Books by
Austin McK. Francis**

A Company of Anglers
editor (1998)

Smart Squash II
(1994)

Sparse Grey Hackle
editor (1993)

Catskill Rivers
(1983)

Smart Squash I
(1977)

Catskill Flytier
coauthored with
Harry Darbee
(1977)

A/P   Brook Trout   Gordon Allen

The story behind these two etchings is that Gordon Allen, fishing on what he presumed was public water on the upper Beaverkill, was apprehended by Dave Hoag, caretaker of the Balsam Lake Club, on whose water Allen was actually fishing. Jim Dudley, club president, happened to be in residence, and upon questioning Allen, judged him to be of good character and invited him to continue fishing the club's water. Months later, the artist's proofs of Allen's sketches arrived with a thank-you note for Dudley's forbearance and hospitality.

Courtesy Elisabeth Dudley,
photographs by Steve Wisbauer.

Beaverkill River, above Cooks Falls.
It was a Fall afternoon—the time of year when nature starts to weave her tapestry of glorious colors, creating purplish hues over the woodland, and scattering her seeds over the earth to begin a new cycle.
—JOSHUA GEROW

Land of Little Rivers

A Story in Photos of Catskill Fly Fishing

AUSTIN McK. FRANCIS

Photography by Enrico Ferorelli

THE  BEAVERKILL PRESS

DISTRIBUTED BY W.W. NORTON & COMPANY, NEW YORK

All photographs are copyrighted by the respective photographers.
Photograph credits are given for supplemental photography only. All other
photographs are by Enrico Ferorelli.

Book design: Katy Homans
River map illustrations: John Manikowski
River map coloring: Mita Corsini Bland
Sepia drawings: Mita Corsini Bland
Copperplate etchings: Gordon Allen

Library of Congress Catalog Card Number: 99-640926

Beaverkill Press gratefully acknowledges the support of
Brent R. Nicklas, who financed the printing of *Land of Little Rivers*.

Printed in Italy by Stamperia Valdonega
First printing

For John McDonald . . .
American angling's finest scholar.

John McDonald, 1906–1998
Photograph by Larry Robins.

Acknowledgments

For helping to make *Land of Little Rivers,* I would like to thank the following:

Enrico Ferorelli, whose technical expertise, imagination, and love of fly fishing came together felicitously in creating the beautiful photographs for this book.

The river guides for Enrico: **Bill Kelly, Adrian LaSorte, Bill Ohnemus, Ed Ostapczuk, Rich Post, Chuck Schwartz, Judd Weisberg.**

Roger Lynker for taking us up in his plane to shoot the aerials.

For permission to take photographs: **Balsam Lake Club, Beaverkill Trout Club, Big Bend Club, Clear Lake Club, DeBruce Fly Fishing Club, Fly Fishers Club of Brooklyn, Furlough Lodge, Salmo Fontinalis, Sand Pond, Winnisook Club, Wintoon Waters, The Woman Flyfishers Club.**

For their hospitality while shooting on location: **Gioia and Mitchell Brock, Ed Eckel, Mary and Kingdon Gould, Jr., Vicky and Jim Linville, Herb Shultz.**

Supplemental photographers: **Aerial Views, Inc., Mark Batur, Bruce Curtis, Henry G. Davis, Bruce Fizzell, Scott Foster, Richard Franklin, Leslie Gill, Kris Lee, Grant McClintock, Linda Morgens, Ed Pfizenmaier, Larry Robins, Cleve Speer, Joan Sydlow, Page Waller, Sandra Weiner, Ricker Winsor, Steve Wisbauer.**

For family photographs: **Mary Dette Clark, Melvin Eck, Judie Darbee Vinciguerra.**

For the hatchery chapter: **Alan Mack, Lisa Shaver and Kayla.**

Joan Wulff and the **Wulff Fishing School.**

John Manikowski for illustrating the maps; **Mita Corsini Bland** for coloring them and for her sepia drawings; **Gordon Allen** for his brook trout and mayfly etchings.

Nikki LaBranche for fine art research and consulting.

At the American Museum of Fly Fishing: **Sean Sonderman, Gary Tanner, Sara Wilcox.**

At the Catskill Fly Fishing Center: **Kathy Bryant, Lisa Lyons.**

At the Anglers' Club of New York: **Nancy Moore, Mary O'Malley.**

Judith and **Jim Bowman,** for helping with the literature chapter.

For historical fact-checking and research support: **Jim Brown, Hoagy Carmichael, Dave Catizone, Robert Titus, Ed Van Put.**

Katy Homans for book production planning and coordination, and for her elegant book design.

Jill Mason for meticulous, intelligent copyediting.

Our printer, Stamperia Valdonega, Verona, Italy: **Martino Mardersteig, Sue Medlicott, Massimo Tonolli.**

Our distributor, W.W. Norton: **Star Lawrence, Bill Rusin, Vic Schmalzer.**

Ted Miller for legal counsel and setting up the structure of Beaverkill Press.

Paul Schmookler and **Ingrid Sills** for sharing their publishing and marketing expertise.

Jennifer Prosek for her ebullient energy and skillful direction of our publicity program.

Nancy Becce Lewis, Beaverkill Press manager and wearer of some thirty hats, for her wry wit, and for maintaining order in the face of chaos.

And most of all my wife, **Ross Francis,** for her pride in my passion.

Contents

Fishing in the Mountains, **Thomas Doughty, oil on panel, c.1840.**

Holding true to Catskill type, the land was one of beautiful combinations. Hill met valley in a succession of soft curves. Brooks poured into the mother stream from little gorges. Hemlocks darkened the watercourses, and the farther ranges shone with maple, ash, and oak. Toward the east the larger mountains looked very blue in the chastened light. There lurked still much of the aboriginal mystery in the forest dimness. Everything was so quiet that one could almost hear the mumbling of the Fates.—T. MORRIS LONGSTRETH

Foreword

~~~~~~~~~~~~~~~~~~~~~~~~~~~~~~~~~~~~

There is, in my experience, no mistaking the Catskill mountains and rivers for anyplace else on earth. Perhaps it's simply that I learned to fly-fish on those rivers—the Willowemoc, the Beaverkill, the branches of the Delaware and its main stem alike, waters as different from each other as the Catskills themselves are from the Rockies or the Sierra Nevada. And yet so keenly are we anglers of place—the weight of the countryside bearing down on us midstream— that anyone who fishes the Catskill rivers soon recognizes the affinities between them, without perhaps being able to say what those affinities are. Wherever you come from, you cross a rise on the road to Livingston Manor or Roscoe or Hancock, and you are suddenly there, in the Catskills, never mind how much "there" differs from itself.

The mood of these rivers has to do with the way the hills shoulder up to the water's edge, leaving only a band of sky above you, and with the way the river bends cut off the view both upstream and down. Even if you fish with friends here, it is common in the Catskills to be over- come by a sense of isolation, not just the solitude we all come looking for, but something a little beyond solitude, a sense of otherness. Again, this is a feature of the topography, the fact that sometimes the only level clearing in sight is the one you're wading in. It has to do as well with the way some rivers—I think especially of the Delaware—surrender them- selves only at dark, when fishing is wholly a matter of judging between shadow and less shadow and the only light left in the sky is the little that remains on the water.

It's possible to be a fly fisher, I suppose, without taking an interest in the history of fly fishing. It depends on whether a sense of the past enriches, for you, your sense of the moment. But if, while fishing the Beaverkill in spring, you take a dark Hendrickson from your fly box, you might stop to consider all the ways there are to consider that fly— its resemblance to the naturals, its appearance to the trout, and so on. But ask yourself this, too. How did that one representation of *Ephemerella subvaria*—among all possible representations—win out? When anglers talk about the culture of fly fishing, they tend to mean its art, its literature, and the singular work of singular craftsmen and women—rodbuilders, reelmakers, flytiers. But part of what the culture of fly fishing means is this: We do not fish in a world of unlimited choices. We adhere to conventions with deep roots, whether we know it or not. Part of the pleasure of fly fishing is knowing it.

It has been hotly said, and hotly denied, that American fly fishing began in the Catskills. As a matter of strict precedence it is probably true. As a matter of influence it is certainly true. The most influential school of split-cane rodbuilding in this country modeled its rods on the requirements of Catskill rivers. And, far more important, a lineage of flytiers, from Theodore Gordon to the Darbees and the Dettes, virtually defined the character of the American dry fly. Countless flies, first propagated in the vises of Catskill tiers, made their way to America's other great fishing grounds, where they were adapted to local needs, much as Gordon adapted Halford's flies. In the Catskills, the great flies of the Catskill tradition are still great flies. They look terrific, match the hatches, and catch lots of fish.

It's natural to wonder about the birthplace of American fly fishing, but I have often wondered where it will mature. *Land of Little Rivers* is, in a sense, a book about the maturity of American fly fishing, about a place—the Catskills—where the weight of accumulated experience is great enough to persuade an attentive angler that he or she is fishing across time. These rivers have seen it all—wildness, overfishing, industrialization, devastation, flood, drought, dams, and fashion—and yet they persist in drawing anglers. The white heat of American fly fishing has moved west in the past two or three decades, to Montana, for one. Or perhaps it's more accurate to say that the white heat of American fly fishing has moved everywhere. But that is the paradox of the Catskills. They are a memory, a rich historical and cultural memory, and yet they are as vital as they ever were. Both the memory and the vitality are present in this book.

If you have never fished the Catskills, *Land of Little Rivers* will serve as a primer not to the techniques but to the spirit in which these waters should be fished. And if you have fished the Catskills, this book will remind you, every time you open it, why you do and how much you owe to those who fished here before you and to those who will fish here after you.

Verlyn Klinkenborg

Introduction

~~~~~~

This book has been given to me as a vessel to fill.

After thirty years of immersion in the lives of those who have been here before us, I have come to realize that the Catskills is a place of the spirit. The Indians who lived here thousands of years ago understood this collectively. Since then, individuals have come along who understood it each in ways that were given to them. They are here in this book, from Norris, to Gordon, McDonald, Darbee, and the rest.

In author Norman Maclean's family, "there was no clear line between religion and fly fishing," and I think I finally am understanding that it's not a way of worshipping or even of simple reverence, but a way of taking hold and giving back. Of returning what has been given.

For the Lenni Lenape tribe of the Algonquians, Manitou inhabited the Onti Ora, the Mountains of the Sky, here in the Catskills. Manitou is a supernatural power that permeates the world, possessed in varying degrees by both spiritual and human beings. I know this is a bit strong for many of us, but it was out there for them and it is out there still.

I believe it is this power—call it passion, dedication, commitment, vision, love, or what you will—that has inspired the myriad fly fishers who in small ways and large have created, fought for, and extended a great sporting tradition in a hallowed land, and I respect the honor of presenting them, their feats, and their little rivers in these pages.

Austin McK. Francis
Beaverkill, New York
September 1, 1999

ONE

Catskill Fly Fishing Center

A s home to one of the world's richest fly-fishing traditions, the Catskills were destined to have a museum and center dedicated to the preservation and celebration of our sport. Elsie Darbee started thinking and talking about it back in the seventies, and when the museum began in 1978, she was chosen as the first president.

The Catskill Fly Fishing Center's museum, administration offices, gift shop, education building, pavilion, and casting pond reside on its thirty-five-acre site bordering Willowemoc Creek.

The little museum was incorporated in 1981 as the Catskill Fly Fishing Center, Inc., and began life in the same Roscoe, New York, movie house where Walt Dette and Harry Darbee started their fly-tying careers in the 1930s. Gradually, through a series of fund-raising dinners and campaigns, and with the help of Jimmy Carter and Paul Volcker, both avid anglers, the Center purchased in 1983 a thirty-five-acre site on Willowemoc Creek, built a steel access bridge to the site, renovated a farmhouse and barn to house the museum, gift shop, and educational programs. Then in 1995, capping a successful $400,000 fund drive, the Center opened its new museum building, having hired Lisa Lyons the year before as the first full-time museum director.

A distinguishing feature of the Catskill Fly Fishing Center is its education programs. For example, summer conservation camps, begun in 1988, are held each July for campers from eight to eighteen years old. Taught by high-school science teachers and experienced fly fishers, youngsters learn the principal angling skills with particular emphasis on how good fishing depends on healthy streams and healthy streams depend on environmentally sensitive anglers (and non-anglers). Another education program, "The River in Our Backyard," consists of a ten-week course given for local third graders, taught by volunteers, and covers

CFFC's museum accommodates permanent and changing exhibitions, receptions, and meetings.

Catskill Fly Fishing Center, Inc.
P.O. Box 1295
Livingston Manor, NY 12758
914.439.4810
914.439.3387 fax
www.cffcm.org

CFFC's museum building, designed by Raul de Armas, opened May 28, 1995.

the trout's life cycle, stream insects, flytying, and trout hatchery operations. The Center's education programs are supported by grants and scholarships to needy students.

The future plans of the Catskill Fly Fishing Center include the development of a research center that will offer information resources to writers, photographers, researchers, conservation groups, government agencies, developers (needing limitation data for watershed projects), and others interested in knowing more about fly-responsive fishes and their habitats. In combination with its museum and education programs, the research center will round out the Center's triad mission to **preserve** America's fly-fishing heritage, **teach** its future generations of fly fishers, and **protect** its fly-fishing environments.

Looking north up the Delaware's East Branch at its junction with the Beaverkill, which flows in from the right.
Photograph by Bruce Fizzell.

PART ONE

Rivers

Dry Brook.

TWO

Land of Little Rivers

~~~~~~

In the beginning, water covered everything that is now the Catskills. There were no mountains or rivers, just a flat-bottomed, shallow sea extending past the present Atlantic coastline across the Chesapeake and Delaware channels on up over Pennsylvania and New York into Canada.

Sediments—fine grains and fragments of rocks from older mountains—washed in and settled on the sea bottom, compressing into layers of stratified rock—mostly red, grey, and green sandstones, red and grey shales, and quartz conglomerates.

These rock strata were well embedded when, about 10 million years ago, a series of bucklings in the earth's crust formed the Appalachians.

Instead of taking the peak-and-valley shape of its neighboring strata, the Catskills upheaved from the sea as a level plateau.

Even as the land rose, deep channels were being worn into the rocky strata by subsurface currents and, later, by **giant watercourses occupying the position of and flowing in a direction that corresponded to our present streams.** Thus began the valleys, in whose centers the principal rivers were to carve their beds.

The erosion continued, fed by rains, creating tributaries, smaller brooks, creeks, and then tiny rills etching their way branchlike up onto the peaks of the adolescent mountains. In the 2 million years since, a number of influences have produced today's well-worn mountain range: sideways movements of the earth's crust tilted the strata and gave character here and there to the otherwise flat-layered plateau; **four or five glaciers, the last about thirty-five thousand years ago, left their legacy of gougings, mineral salts, and imported rocks;** plant and animal decay, combined with fine bits of worn-off rocks, made the sandy, gravelly soils in which the native hemlocks and pines were to thrive.

The Catskill mountains occupy about four thousand square miles west of the Hudson River, a little over one hundred miles upstream from the Atlantic. From the

Sepia drawings by Mita Corsini Bland.

33

Hudson, at sea level, the land rises gently to the base of the mountains, about four hundred feet above sea level. From there, the mountains climb sharply to more than three thousand feet in less than a mile.

Dozens of rounded Catskill summits rise to over three thousand feet, and a few giants of the interior range exceed four thousand feet. Compared with Adirondack peaks, which are taller but whose bases lie well above sea level, the Catskills possess a greater vertical relief.

Catskill peaks are a zone of convergence for three precipitation systems that make them one of the most water-rich regions in the country. They stand in the path of southeast winds blowing inland from the ocean. Their heights force the humid air upward, cool it, and draw out its moisture as rain or snow. They are also periodically inundated by cyclonic storms moving up the east coast; winds in advance of these storms blow from the east and dump huge amounts of water when they collide with the Catskills' eastern slopes. When added to the more widespread precipitation caused by low pressure systems, fronts, thunderstorms, and snowstorms, it is easy to understand why the Catskills get so much water.

Water is the Catskills' most valuable resource. It grows the trees that sustained local industries for centuries. It is exported to New York City by the hundreds of millions of gallons daily. And it provides a home for one of the finest freshwater fish populations in the world.

Topographically, the Catskills are a small, well-worn range of mountains, among the oldest in the world. They lack awe-inspiring peaks sculpted by deep ravines. Morris Longstreth, a hiker of the early 1900s, observed that their inherent beauty "resides very little in their measurements, but in the serene sweep of their slopes, the harmony of their contours, and the appeal of their covering, whether it be forest, rock, or snow."

Like the humble mountains whence it flows, the typical Catskill trout stream has been created on a personal scale that intensifies the feelings of privacy and intimacy with nature so prized among anglers. It is the perfect size for fly fishing. Said Louis Rhead of the upper Beaverkill, "Excepting in those rare years when all nature languishes in drought, the stream is broad, deep, and copious. To the fly-caster it is the ideal stream, as he can—after the spring 'fresh' is over—wade the entire stream, excepting at two or three very deep pools and at the falls."

Longstreth was a disciple of John Burroughs, the famed nineteenth-century naturalist and author, who was born on the East Branch of the Delaware River and grew up fishing in the Catskills. His keen sense of observation and eloquence enabled him to create haunting evocations of his native streams:

The creek loves to burrow under the roots of a great tree, to scoop out a pool after leaping over the prostrate trunk of one, and to pause at the foot of a ledge of moss-covered rocks, with ice-cold water dripping down. How straight the current goes for the rock! Note its corrugated, muscular appearance; it strikes and glances off, but accumulates, deepens with well-defined eddies above and to one side; on the edge of these the trout lurk and spring upon their prey.

Fifty or so years before Burroughs, Washington Irving had come back from learning to angle in England and created his own vivid image of Catskill streams:

Our first essay was along a mountain brook among the highlands of the Hudson, a most unfortunate place for the execution of those piscatory tactics which had been invented along the velvet margins of quiet English rivulets. It was one of those wild streams that lavish among our romantic solitudes unheeded beauties enough to fill the sketch-book of a hunter of the picturesque. Sometimes it would leap down rocky shelves, making small cascades over which the trees threw their broad balancing sprays, and long nameless weeds hung in fringes from the impending banks, dripping with diamond drops. Sometimes it would brawl and fret along a ravine in the matted shade of a forest, filling it with murmurs, and after this termagant career would steal forth into open day with the most placid demure face imaginable; as I have seen some pestilent shrew of a housewife, after filling her home with uproar and ill-humor, come dimpling out of doors, swimming and courtseying and smiling upon all the world.

Even without the benefit of large underground springs—like those of England's "quiet rivulets"—the entire Catskill region is a lacework of rivers. **Out of each hollow flows a brook, and fifteen smaller brooks unite to lend it volume** before it has run three miles. Water runs everywhere, and one wonders how it keeps flowing from the ridges without daily replenishment.

It flows from highly absorbent layers of water-bearing sand, gravel, and rock, from countless seeps and smaller springs, from the blotting-pad forest of leaf-mold, mosses, ferns, and trees, themselves living reservoirs. There are also spring holes in the streambeds helping to keep them cooler in summer, warmer and moving in winter, sustaining their flow through the year.

It was Longstreth who—though not an angler—remarked while hiking the Esopus valley in 1915, "Instead of the Mountains of the Sky, the Indians might have called this country the Land of Little Rivers, for down each glen springs some brook to join the bright Esopus. . . . It is for its streams that the Catskills has a right to be ranked with the great family of American parks."

THREE

Beaverkill River

A thousand years ago, or more, two foot trails joined on the upper Beaverkill at Shin Creek; they were used by the Esopus Indians to reach their hunting grounds and were the earliest human penetration of the Catskills, passing through what is still today a wild and remote region.

As late as 1873, when the first fishing club appeared on the river, access to the upper Beaverkill was still primitive; a wagon road came up from Roscoe but stopped at a Shin Creek sawmill. From there to the headwaters was still only a footpath; members of the club found it quicker to come in over the top from the next valley to the east.

Although most trout fishermen today are more familiar with the Beaverkill from Roscoe down to East Branch, the upper Beaverkill was where the trout were in the late 1800s. Any sport fishing then on

Beaverkill Falls (left) was once the site of Jones Mill (above), one of seventeen sawmills operating along the fourteen miles from the falls downstream to Rockland.
Mill photo courtesy the Shaver family.

the lower Beaverkill would have been mainly for black bass. The European brown trout, with its tolerance for the warmer water in the lower rivers, first came to America in 1883 but was not widely established or accepted by Catskill anglers until after 1900.

In 1870 and 1873, two railroads—the Rondout & Oswego on the north and the New York & Oswego Midland on the south—were completed just ten miles on either side of the headwaters of the Rondout, Neversink, Esopus, Willowemoc, and Beaverkill rivers. The R&O gave access to the upper Beaverkill before it had a wagon road up its full length. Fishermen

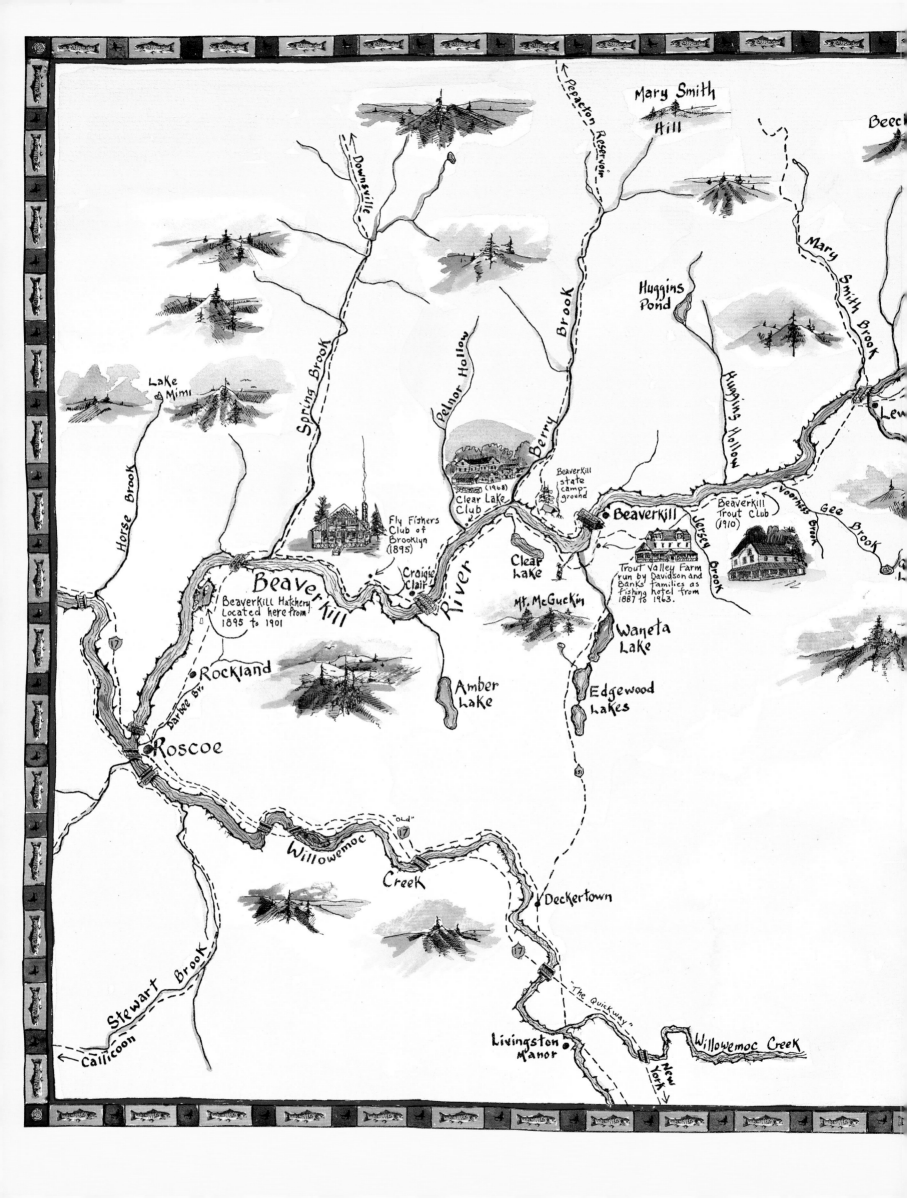

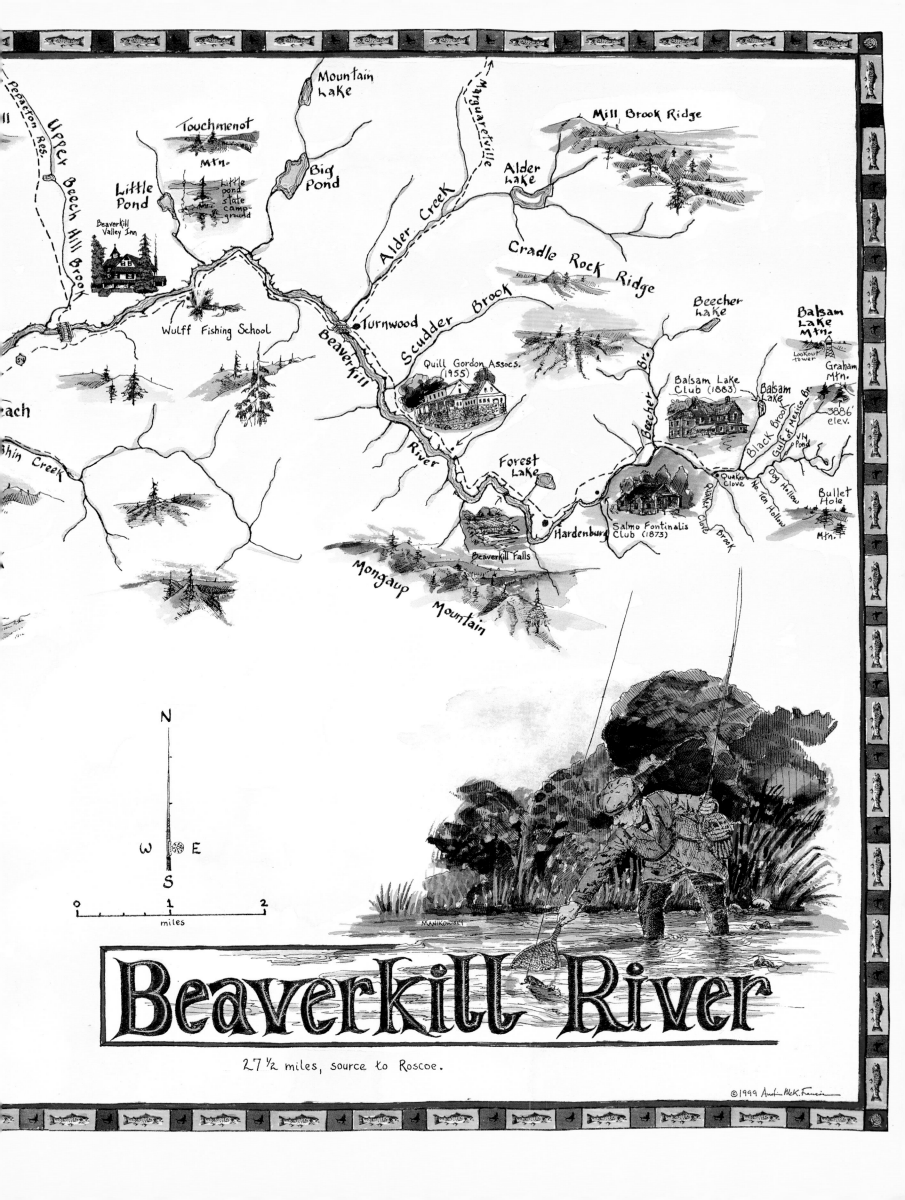

Mountain Lake

Touchmenot Mtn.

Little Pond

Big Pond

little pond state campground

Beaverkill Valley Inn

Wulff Fishing School

Upper Beech Hill Brook

Pepacton Res.

Mill Brook Ridge

Alder Lake

Alder Creek

Maguaretsville

Cradle Rock Ridge

Scudder Brook

Turnwood

Beaverkill River

Quill Gordon Assocs. (1955)

Beecher Lake

Balsam Lake Mtn.

Lookout tower

Graham Mtn.

Balsam Lake Club (1883)

Balsam Lake

Black Brook

Gulf of Mexico Br.

3886' elev.

V/A Pond

Beecher Br.

Bullet Hole Mtn.

Forest Lake

Quaker Clove

No. Ten Hollow

Dog Hollow

Hardenburg

Salmo Fontinalis Club (1873)

Quaker Clove Brook

Beaverkill Falls

Mongaup Mountain

Beech

Shin Creek

MANIKOWSKI

N
W E
S

0   1   2
miles

BeaverKill River

27 ½ miles, source to Roscoe.

©1999 Austin McK. Francis

Trout Valley Farm, in the late 1800s, was operated for seventy-six years as a fisherman's boardinghouse, first by Jay Davidson and then by Fred Banks III. The state bought and torched it in 1963.
Courtesy Patricia and John Adams.

got off at the Arkville station on the East Branch of the Delaware. From there they took a mountain buckboard up Dry Brook to Seager's and then hiked in over Graham Mountain. For the more courageous, there was the "Cat's Ladder," a rough wagon road from Seager's that skirted the other side of the mountain. One of the travelers over this road had this to say: "Its heathenish and unconscionable construction is very destructive, yea even fatal to piety, and therefore it is not only productive of physical and mental torture in this world, but liable to compromise our comfort in the next."

To be an angler in this remote territory in those days required both vigor and determination, evidenced by this May 6, 1897, logbook entry of the Balsam Lake Club:

While going over the top of the mountain, passing the Lover's Leap, the wagon turned completely over twice. We were precipitated over a precipice of some 2685½ feet alighting on the tops of tall trees which we carefully climbed down. Then ascending the mountain we turned the wagon over twice so it would be where it was before our aerial flight, and once more resumed our trip. On arriving at the clubhouse and finding no other members here, we chose the best rooms and have slept under four blankets. Ice formed on the lake at nights, but the days have been pleasantly warm.

As increasing numbers of city fly fishers headed to the Beaverkill, those who weren't members of the new clubs were being welcomed by valley farmers, who opened their houses to visiting anglers. From the top of the river down, a sampling of these newly christened "boardinghouses" included Ransom Weaver, John Slater, Jim Murdock, Ed Sprague, S.A. Voorhess, Mrs. Jersey, and Hank Ellsworth.

"J.M. Johnson telling a fish story, on the Beaverkill, NY"—a group typical of the guests at Jay Davidson's boardinghouse.
Courtesy American Museum of Fly Fishing.

Fred Banks III, proprietor of Trout Valley Farm, holding the kind of trout that brought anglers back year after year to his establishment on the upper Beaverkill.
Courtesy Frederic Banks IV.

The boardinghouses of the Beaverkill were institutions in themselves, combining the services of hotels, chambers of commerce, and fishing outfitters. They ranged from small farms with a spare room to well-organized manor houses that printed illustrated booklets and took in up to fifty guests. Prices in the 1890s were $4 to $7 per week, about $1.25 for overnight, and $.25 for a fisherman's lunch. One-way train fare from New York City ran about $2.50, and the welcoming horse and wagon was on the house.

River View Inn, one of the well-known Beaverkill boardinghouses, was located a mile or so downriver from Roscoe. John Ferdon added a wing to his farmhouse in the 1890s and opened it up as Hillside Summer Home. His son Edwin changed the name to River View Inn to reflect the growing popularity of the lower Beaverkill among trout fishermen. By the 1920s, River View Inn had attracted a following of angling notables the likes of A.E. Hendrickson, Gene Connett, Louis Rhead, Charles Ritz, and George LaBranche, and it buzzed with excitement at the height of each fishing season. In the thirties, Edwin Ferdon's daughter Winnie ran the inn with her new husband, Walt Dette, but along with many similar Catskill establishments it succumbed to the Depression and ceased operations as a boardinghouse in 1933. Having

Larry Rockefeller bought the Bonnie View—formerly a fisherman's boarding-house built in 1895—and restored it as the Beaverkill Valley Inn, part of his upper Beaverkill wilderness-home program. BVI, with its own stretch of the river, caters to anglers, hikers, and outdoor enthusiasts.

(Left) Tiers of log-and-stone dams (see detail below) built using oxen in 1892 by Colonel Charles H. Odell, then owner of the river reach that included Beaverkill Falls. These have resisted the ice and floods that regularly take out most other dams on the river.

already tied and sold flies from the cigar counter at the inn, the Dettes became full-time flytiers.

Trout Valley Farm, situated seven miles upriver from Roscoe in the community of Beaverkill, was a most celebrated Beaverkill boarding-house. Theodore Gordon stayed there for weeks at a time over several summers; he also stayed at River View Inn when he had his mother, Fanny, with him and wanted her to be closer to the conveniences of a larger village. Trout Valley Farm was operated for seventy-six continuous years as a fishing hotel, from 1887 to 1922 by Jay Davidson, and by the Frederic Banks family from 1922 to 1963, when it was sold to the state, which torched it to clear the land. As a note from bygone days, even with its capacity of fifty guests, the rooms of Trout Valley Farm never had locks on the doors.

Frederick White fished at Trout Valley Farm for over twenty-five years, beginning in the 1890s, and witnessed there many of the changes taking place during an era of ferment in American angling. He saw bait fishing fall into disrepute even among local residents; he watched as the first women showed the courage to don boots under their knee-length skirts and wade out into the river; and in 1909 he experienced with some poignancy the coming of the dry fly to Beaverkill village:

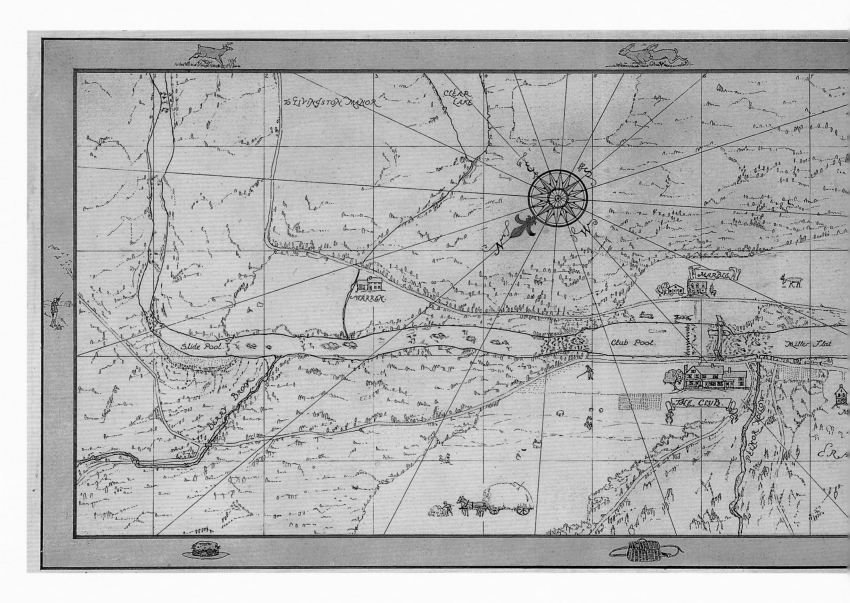

Map drawn by T.M. Bell of the Beaverkill
water of the Jersey Trout Club, later known
as the Iroquois Trout Club and today as the
Clear Lake Club.
Courtesy Catskill Fly Fishing Center.

"Hello, Meester!" A.B. Frost's illustration of
J. Smith, the eponymous spicklefisherman
in Fred White's story of a poacher on the
water of a Beaverkill trout club, who won
the heart of the member who was about to
kick him off the river.

"HELLO, MEESTER!"

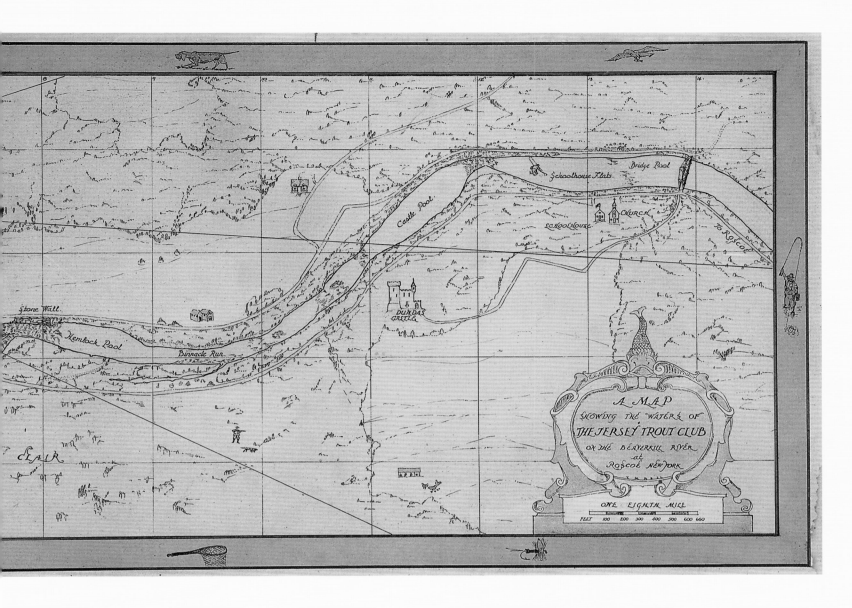

Dr. R.E. Brown arrived one day with an assortment of #14 and #16 midges fresh from England. I happened to be fishing the Bridge pool with a wet fly while the trout were feeding where the current turns into the quieter water of the pool, but they would not take. Dr. Brown stood beside me and in fifteen minutes pulled out five fish from 12 inches to 14 inches with his little floaters much to his gratification and my own chagrin.

Other inns favored by turn-of-the-century Beaverkill anglers included the **Roscoe House,** torn down when the four-lane highway went through in the early sixties. Its owner, William Keener, was an insatiable fly fisherman who for many years held the apocryphal state record for an 8½-pound brook trout caught in 1908 out of the Punchbowl on the hill above Roscoe. No one is sure who fabricated the story.

The **Bonnie View,** a large Victorian house set at the river's edge on the upper Beaverkill above Lew Beach—for nearly a hundred years an unassuming fisherman's boardinghouse—has been reborn as the Beaverkill Valley Inn, an upscale, well-appointed river hotel with its own trout water.

And then there was the **Antrim Lodge,** formerly Central House, in Roscoe, whose downstairs bar and common room are famous in angling

(Above) The Beaverkill Covered Bridge. In the far background beyond the bridge, a small stream comes into the head of the pool where Harry Darbee caught his first big trout, a seventeen-inch brown, on a ten-foot bilberry switch and a grasshopper when he was eleven years old.
Photograph by Kris Lee.

(Left) Shin Creek, home fishing grounds of Bill Hardie, who in 1856 delivered a live, five-pound brook trout to P.T. Barnum's New York City museum-aquarium, collected Barnum's $190 reward, and left town only to have the trout die the next morning. Hardie had secretly kept the trout alive by giving it "a good ol' raftsman's hooter of Sullivan County redeye."
Photograph by Bruce Fizzell.

literature. It was the setting of Keener's Pool, a.k.a. the Antrim Bar, where many Beaverkill anglers went to continue their "fishing" when they came off the river. The most monstrous of trout taken out of the Beaverkill were landed at Keener's Pool. The Antrim is closed now, its exterior festooned with peeling paint, its bar abandoned and covered with dust, a sign not so much of a declining thirst in après-fishing as of a change in the life-style of anglers.

* * *

By 1900, the upper Beaverkill had been transformed into a largely posted, private river. A combination of fly-fishing clubs and individual owners bought or leased almost all the fishing rights from the headwaters down to the village of Beaverkill. There, Trout Valley Farm still catered to the public, but below Beaverkill private ownership extended the rest of the way down to Rockland, leaving only a couple of miles of unposted water before the river joined the Willowemoc at Junction Pool.

Unless a fisherman knew one of the new owners or was a member or guest of one of the half-dozen clubs, there was no longer any legal way

Beaverkill Ri

15 ½ miles, Roscoe to East Branch.

©1999 Austin McK. Francis

MANIKOWSKI

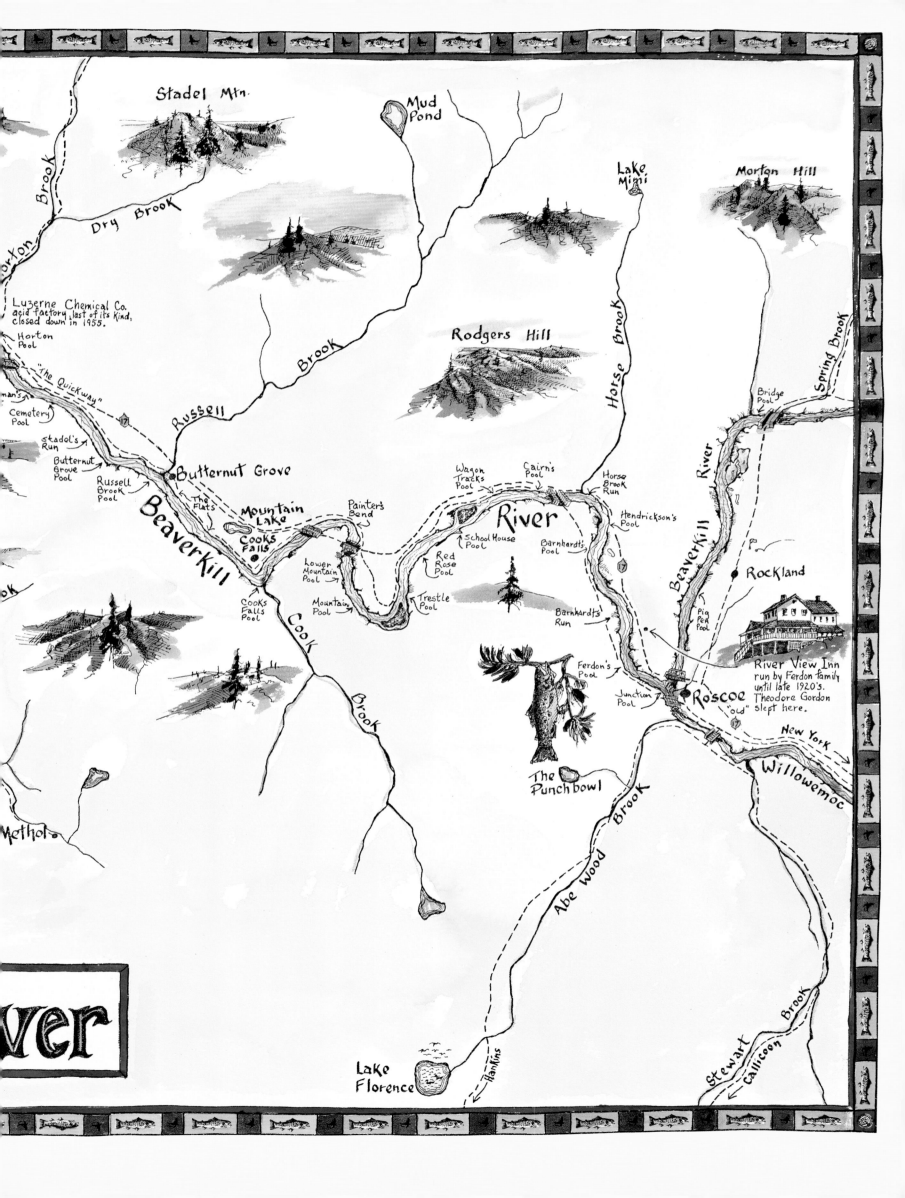

Stadel Mtn.

Mud Pond

Lake Mimi

Morton Hill

Brook

Dry Brook

Luzerne Chemical Co.
acid factory, last of its kind,
closed down in 1955.

Rodgers Hill

Horse Brook

Spring Brook

Horton
Pool

"The Quickway"

Russell

Brook

Bridge
Pool

Cemetery
Pool

17

Stadol's
Run

Butternut Grove

Wagon
Tracks
Pool

Cairn's
Pool

Horse
Brook
Run

Hendrickson's
Pool

Beaverkill River

Butternut
Grove
Pool

Russell
Brook
Pool

The Flats

Mountain
Lake

Painter's
Bend

River

School House
Pool

Barnhardt's
Pool

Rockland

Beaverkill

Cooks
Falls

Lower
Mountain
Pool

Red
Rose
Pool

7

Pig
Pen
Pool

Cooks
Falls
Pool

Mountain
Pool

Trestle
Pool

Barnhardt's
Run

River View Inn
run by Ferdon family
until late 1920's.
Theodore Gordon
"old" slept here.

Cook

Brook

Ferdon's
Pool

Junction
Pool

Roscoe

New York

The
Punchbowl

Willowemoc

Methol

Abe Wood Brook

Stewart

Callicoon Brook

ver

Lake
Florence

Hankins

Dappled in early spring sunlight, this sign once stood, until appropriated by a secret admirer, at the iron bridge crossing the last few hundred feet of the upper Beaverkill before it enters Junction Pool.

Photograph by Richard Franklin.

(Left) Junction Pool, home of the Beamoc (above), the mythical trout with two antlered heads and a beaver's tail. Confused by the sharply converging currents of the Beaverkill and Willowemoc, the Beamoc can't decide which stream to swim up, so he lives out his days in Junction Pool. Conceived by Harry Darbee and depicted here by Reginald Todhunter, he now is the symbol for the local Beamoc Chapter of Trout Unlimited.
Beamoc drawing courtesy Catskill Fly Fishing Center, gift of Judie Darbee Vinciguerra.

to fish the upper Beaverkill. Thus, Catskill anglers of the twentieth century necessarily turned their attention to the lower Beaverkill, or the "Big River," as many of them began calling it, and today, with more than one hundred years of added tradition and publicity, it is this part of the river that writers have in mind when they speak of "the most celebrated trout river in the world."

To achieve its preeminence, the lower Beaverkill of course had to remain open to all fishermen, and for this the angling public owes its gratitude to one man, Lithgow Osborne. As recalled by Sparse Grey Hackle, "When Osborne was the State's Conservation Commissioner back in the thirties, each year he took a little of the Catskill anglers' license fees and devoted [the money] to a most sagacious and forward-looking use—he bought up fishing rights of private landowners along the north bank of the river; the south bank was already owned by the railroad, which had never prevented fishermen from clambering down over its tracks to the river. I doubt if he ever paid as much as $100 to any one landowner. It would be worth a million or more today, I'm sure."

Including the fishing rights Osborne bought on the Willowemoc between Livingston Manor and Roscoe, this twenty-three-mile stretch of river is the only uninterrupted public fishing water of appreciable size in the Catskills.

THE HILLSIDE SUMMER HOME
ROSCOE, N.Y.

Altitude 1500 ft.

(Above) Centerfold from a brochure for John Ferdon's Hillside Summer Home in Roscoe, near Junction Pool.
Courtesy Mary Dette Clark.

(Right) An unusual day at Cairns' Pool, which is usually crowded with fishermen.
Photograph by Grant McClintock.

(Below) A.E. Hendrickson, after whom Roy Steenrod named the Hendrickson fly, and his fishing pals Dr. J.S. Chaffee (center) and George Stevenson (right), displaying their catch from a day on the lower Beaverkill, on the porch of River View Inn (formerly Hillside Summer Home) in 1920.
Courtesy Mary Dette Clark.

With all the right ingredients—easy access to a big, beautiful river full of large brown trout and surrounded by friendly innkeepers—the lower Beaverkill began accumulating the store of characters and legends that have made it unique in angling history.

Although the lower Beaverkill attracts even more anglers than it did in Theodore Gordon's day, old-timers will tell you that the fishing will never be as good as it was back in the golden era. Certainly a lot has changed, and—regardless of the state of current fishing—one naturally grows nostalgic when talking about the good old days of Catskill angling.

There was a time when, arriving in Roscoe, you could buy the right fly at every store in town except the undertaker's. A diligent salesman from William Mills & Son in New York had made the rounds of the jeweler, the dry-goods man, the druggist, everybody, and impressed on each merchant his role in supporting the proud reputation of the Beaverkill.

Opening Day of trout season authenticates each year the Beaverkill's

Another view of Cairns' Pool, with the pathway for disabled access coming down from the right. **Project Access,** *begun by Joan Stoliar in 1985, is dedicated "to making prime trout fishing streams accessible to elderly and disabled anglers." In the Catskills, nine pathways have been built on the Beaverkill, Willowemoc, and Neversink and are maintained by members of Theodore Gordon Flyfishers, Trout Unlimited, and the Catskill Fly Fishing Center.*

(Left) Trestle Pool, beneath the old O&W Railroad bridge, on the lower Beaverkill just upriver from Mountain Pool.

(Below) Upper Mountain Pool, just above the spot where Sparse Grey Hackle set the tale of his fight with a fifty-pound brown trout, armed only with a loaf of bread and a case of Scotch.

hallowed position among trout rivers. In spite of the usually raw weather and turbid waters, hordes of anglers make the annual pilgrimage, ignoring the odds against catching anything but pneumonia. Indeed, they return more to observe a ritual and renew tradition than they do to catch trout. Only Red Smith, the king of sports columnists, could capture its ineffable nature:

> *One stormy April night three men rode out of the darkness into the streets of the Catskills village of Roscoe. "Gentlemen," said Sparse Grey Hackle, "remove your hats. This is it."*
>
> *"This is where the trout was invented?" the driver asked.*
>
> *"Oh," Mr. Hackle said, "he existed in a crude, primitive form in Walton's England—"*
>
> *"But this," said Mead Schaeffer, artist and angler, "is where they painted spots on him and taught him to swim."*
>
> *It was the eve of Opening Day of the New York trout season. It can be said without irreverence that to celebrate Opening Day on the Beaverkill is a little like observing Christmas in Bethlehem. For the Beaverkill is the shrine, the fountainhead, the most beloved and best-known trout stream in America, the river of George LaBranche, Theodore Gordon, Guy Jenkins and the Fly Fishers Club of Brooklyn.*

FOUR

Willowemoc Creek

~~~~~~

In the 1870s, when railroads opened up the Catskills to visiting fishermen, Willowemoc Creek became a tender bit of accessible remoteness. It beckoned and the anglers followed.

New Yorkers rose early, bundled their gear and lunch, and jumped the ferry to Weehawken, New Jersey. There they took a 7:35 A.M. New York & Oswego Midland train at the foot of Jay Street. It ran up the Hudson River to Cornwall, then turned westward through Middletown, Monticello, and Liberty, arriving at Livingston Manor on the Willowemoc at 12:48 P.M.

Pushing on to the upper river, they took a 1:30 mail stage from the Manor, which deposited them around 4:00 in the village of Willowemoc, where they were met by Mr. Horatio Smith in his buckboard. From there Smith drove them to his boardinghouse on Lake Willowemoc, arriving in time for his guests to wash up and have a short fish before supper. The cost of such outings, in 1890, was $14.81, which included both the train and stage round-trip fares plus board for one week at Mr. Smith's.

J.D. Benham and his friend George Hand stayed at Horatio Smith's in August 1890 and fished the upper Willowemoc. George had never caught a trout before, and he wasn't much of an outdoorsman, but he "caught on" to twelve nice trout, as well as about all the old roots and logs he could find. The last day of their visit, J.D. and George caught thirteen in about twenty minutes, all good-sized fish. George was champion with a twelve-incher. "We could have taken a hundred and thirteen if we had wanted them," said J.D. A lot of small fish was the rule. Earlier that year, Mr. Smith and a companion caught two hundred trout in three hours, eighty of them from one bend in the stream.

The next community downstream, DeBruce, is rich in fly-fishing history. It was there at the mouth of Mongaup Creek around 1899 that George LaBranche cast his first dry fly, "due more to the exigency of the occasion than to any predevised plan for attempting the feat." From his

The Vantran Covered Bridge, below Livingston Manor, was saved from replacement by a concrete span and restored in 1985.

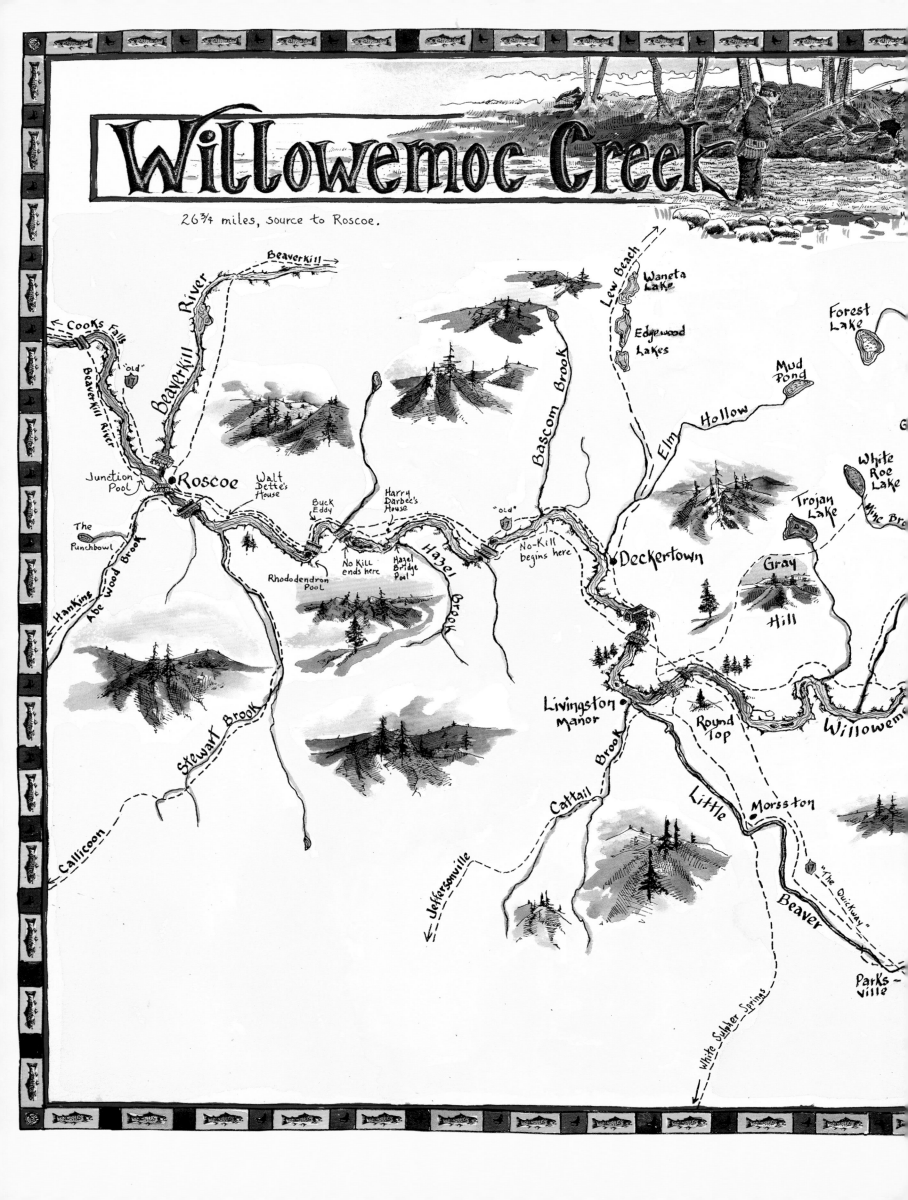

Willowemoc Creek

26¾ miles, source to Roscoe.

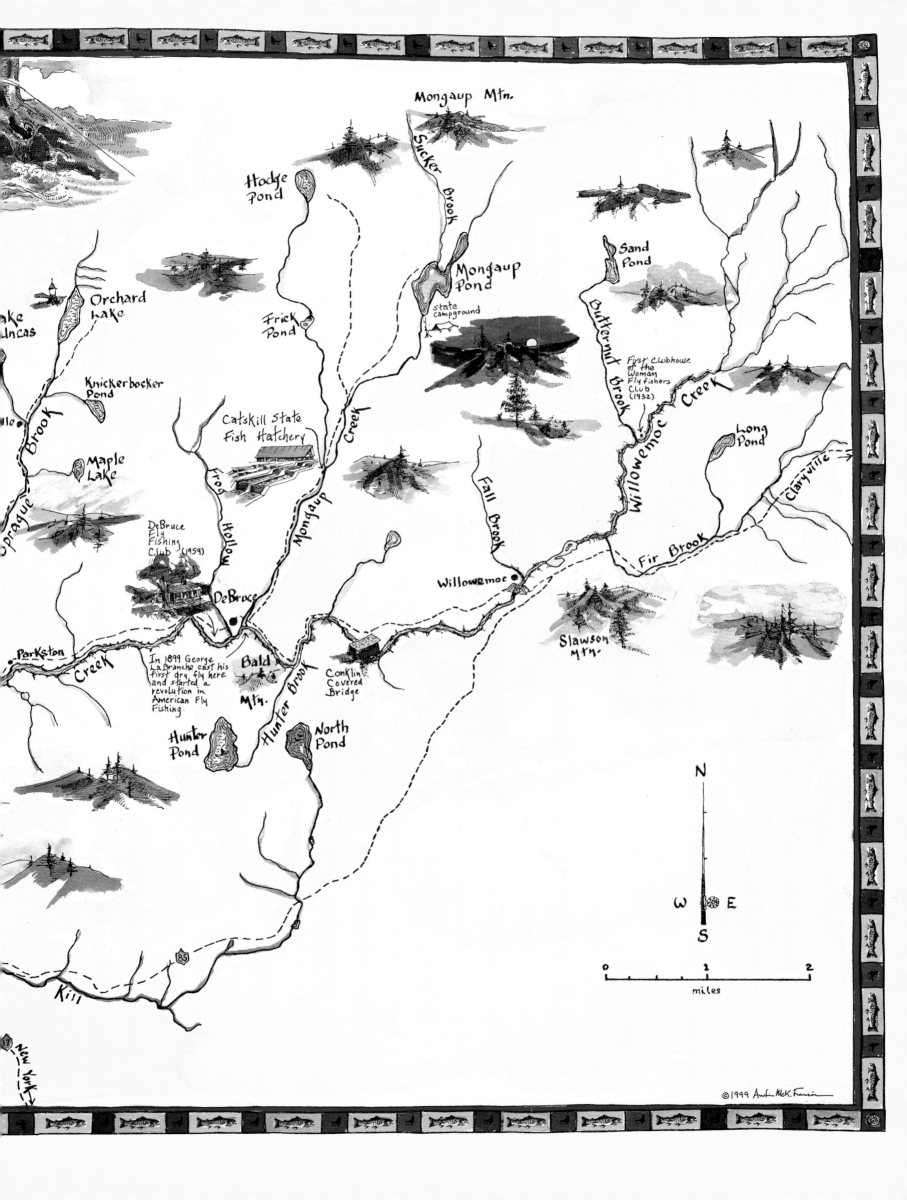

Mongaup Mtn.

Sucker Brook

Hodge Pond

Mongaup Pond

state campground

Sand Pond

Orchard Lake

Lake Uncas

Frick Pond

Butternut Brook

First Clubhouse of the Woman Fly fishers Club (1932)

Willowemoc Creek

Knickerbocker Pond

Sprague Brook

Catskill State Fish Hatchery

Long Pond

Maple Lake

Frost Hollow

Mongaup Creek

Fall Brook

Fir Brook

Claryville

DeBruce Fly Fishing Club (1959)

DeBruce

Willowemoc

Parkston

Creek

In 1899 George La Branche cast his first dry fly here and started a revolution in American Fly Fishing.

Bald Mtn.

Conklin Covered Bridge

Slawson Mtn.

Hunter Brook

Hunter Pond

North Pond

N

W   E

S

0   1   2
miles

85

Kill

New York

©1999 Austin McK. Francis

(Above) Charles B. Ward's DeBruce Club
Inn, a carriage-trade fishing hotel, offered
golf, tennis, and several miles of the choicest
water on the upper Willowemoc. Home of
the Pink Lady cocktail and the Pink Lady
fly, the DeBruce Club Inn was a favorite of
the Anglers' Club for its outings throughout
the 1930s and 1940s.
Courtesy Department of Environmental
Conservation and Ed Van Put.

(Right) The no-kill stretch below Hazel's
Bridge, Harry Darbee's "home pool" just
downhill from his and Elsie's house.
Photograph by Grant McClintock.

house next to the junction of these two streams, he began working out
the theories that he articulated in 1914 in *The Dry Fly and Fast Water*.
LaBranche was also a member of the Beaverkill Trout Club.

George LaBranche and Ed Hewitt used to own a stretch of the
Willowemoc above DeBruce. In an interesting switch on the then current habit of farmers selling their fishing rights and keeping their land,
Hewitt and LaBranche sold their entire Willowemoc property but
retained personal fishing rights for the rest of their lives.

During the early 1900s, in the heyday of Catskill resort hotels, there
were two recipes for Pink Ladies around DeBruce. One called for pale
pink floss ribbed with gold tinsel, duck wings, ginger hackle and tail, all
on a No. 12 hook. It was one of George LaBranche's favorite dry flies.
The other recipe called for gin, apple brandy, lemon juice, grenadine,
and egg white, shaken strenuously with cracked ice and strained into a
tall-stemmed glass. It was a favorite drink of the sporting clientele at
Charles B. Ward's DeBruce Club Inn.

One wants very much to believe the story of a voluptuous blonde
guest at Ward's back in the Roaring Twenties who, on her first attempt at
angling, anointed her Pink Lady in her Pink Lady and caught a monstrous, bibulous trout. Apocryphal, no doubt.

Sand Pond, site of the first private fishing club in the Catskills, was owned for eighty years by the Van Norden family. In 1935, Warner Van Norden built the log-and-stone cabin on the rise at the far end of the lake.
Photograph by the author.

Mr. Ward ran a carriage-trade fishing establishment. The DeBruce Club Inn had tennis courts and a nine-hole golf course, but it was set up mainly for fishing. Gene Connett, proprietor of the Derrydale Press, known for its deluxe limited editions of sporting books, stayed at Ward's regularly. "The Willowemoc is one of the most charming trout streams," he said. "Its variety of water is almost unlimited, and there is a really comfortable inn at DeBruce where the angler is accorded that patient consideration of meals at almost any hour, served by maids who can actually smile."

In the early years of the inn, servants met guests at the door, took care of their horses, and carried their luggage up to enormous rooms with big brass beds. Or they might have been escorted, as Dick Salmon used to say, "to one of the brown-shingled guest cottages dappled about the inn." The meals were fresh country food, deliciously prepared, and generously heaped. The next morning, by fishing time, one's rod would have been taken out of its case, assembled, and hung on a peg next to one's own locker in the tackle room. There were no beats. With several miles of water, and genteel angling companions, there was plenty of

fishing to go around. At sundown, it sometimes got crowded in the tackle room as fishermen vied for benches to unlace boots, get out of waders, and gather in front of the big open fire in the common room.

Ward sold the DeBruce Club Inn in the late 1940s, and the new owner continued to operate it in the old tradition. However, along with many other Catskill hotels in the 1950s, it suffered a continuing loss of business and had to close in 1960. The year before, a group of its regulars including the new owner formed the DeBruce Fly Fishing Club. They leased the stream rights from a fellow member and fitted out one of Ward's old brown-shingled guest cottages as a clubhouse. The inn itself was torn down and sold for timber in 1970.

* * *

If rivers could emote, the Willowemoc would surely envy the Beaverkill. Where they join, the Willowemoc gives up its name to its nobler twin. But why should *it* be the tributary when, before they were named, the Willowemoc was every mile as good a trout river? Not only that, "Whelenaughwemack" was the river's original name all the way down to East Branch, and the Great Beaverkill ending at what is now Roscoe was

its northern tributary—as revealed through Ed Van Put's research for his book *The Beaverkill.*

Whelenaughwemack was the Lenni Lenape Indian's word for "the kettle that washes itself clean," derived from the annual scourings by floods of the river's bed and banks. The Beaverkill got its name from the European settlers impressed by the myriad colonies of "beeves" inhabiting its headwaters.

The Beaverkill River dominated its sister stream because it was destined for greater fame and protection. Already by 1869, the celebrated nature writer John Burroughs stepped out onto its bank and proclaimed:

> *Hail to the Beaverkill!*
>
> *How shall I describe that wild, beautiful stream, with features so like those of all other mountain streams? And yet, as I saw it in the deep twilight of those woods on that June afternoon, with its steady, even flow, and its tranquil, many-voiced murmur, it made an impression upon my mind distinct and peculiar, fraught in an eminent degree with the charm of seclusion and remoteness.*

What began as a trickle grew to a torrent as outdoor writers followed each other in embellishing the reputation of an already famous river. "Uncle Thad" Norris, Robin Ruff, Ben Bent, Frank Forester, Louis Rhead, William A. Bradley, Frederick White, Arnold Gingrich, Red Smith, Sparse Grey Hackle. Can you imagine Sparse naming his wife "Lady Willowemoc"?

The name itself evolved painfully over the years: Whelewaughwemack, Weelewaughwemack, Weelewaughmack, Wilenawemack, Williwernock, Willerwhemack, Williwemauk, Williwemock, Willowemock, Willowemoc. Even that is too cumbersome for stylish anglers: they come and go, speaking of the "Willow." But you will not hear them confuse or shorten the other one. It has only been Beaver Kill, Beaver-kill, or Beaverkill.

As for protection, the upper Beaverkill was never a thoroughfare, even in the late 1800s when a wagon trail came into the head of its valley over Graham Mountain from Seager on Dry Brook. Soon after the turn of the century, a rough motor road was completed from the lower river up to the headwaters. The wagon trail grew over from disuse, and the upper Beaverkill remained a secluded angling paradise of large land holdings, fly-fishing clubs, and privately owned river mileage.

By contrast, the Willowemoc has always been very accessible by rail or road along its lower seven miles between Livingston Manor and Roscoe. The next fifteen miles upriver have from the earliest sport fishing days been paralleled by a rough road through DeBruce, Willowemoc, and up Fir Brook into the Neversink valley.

As a result, the Willowemoc got chopped up into smaller parcels, and except for the Ward estate and a few other longer stretches higher up, it sprouted into a patchwork of hotels, boardinghouses, bungalow colonies, summer camps, sanitariums, and campsites. In the 1950s, the hotels and inns declined and gave way to even smaller lots, vacation cabins, and trailer homes.

It is unfair to suggest that the Willowemoc is a steady procession of unsightly development. There are beautiful, unspoiled sections of the river, both public and private, which run away from the road and through more sparsely populated parts of the valley. Conversely, the Beaverkill valley has eyesores of its own. Moreover, the differences between these two rivers cannot be proven to have influenced the selection of their names. To a fisherman, the notoriety of his stream is secondary to its productivity. He can even tolerate a trailer or two if he is catching fish. And in this regard, the Willowemoc has no reason to be envious at all.

(Right) Dr. Leo Flood and Sparse Grey Hackle at their DeBruce Fly Fishing Club, on whose water Mongaup Creek joins the Willowemoc (below), the setting where George LaBranche cast his first dry fly "due more to the exigency of the occasion than to any predevised plan for attempting the feat."

Lower end of the Overpass Pool above
Vantran bridge, where big cannibal browns
used to lie in its five-foot depths when there
was a chicken factory just upstream. They're
still there, just more dependent on the supply
of natural, and artificial, flies.

(Right) Rhododendron Pool, upstream from
Roscoe, produced a nineteen-inch brown for
the photographer several years ago.
Photograph by Richard Franklin.

Leroy's Pool, West Branch of the Neversink, named after Bruce Leroy, a fishing companion of Theodore Gordon; also the Connell family's favorite spot for swimming, picnicking, and fishing.

Courtesy the Connell family.

FIVE

Neversink River

John Burroughs quickened his pace as he and three friends climbed up the valley of the "Big Injin" and crossed over onto the West Branch of the Neversink. On this June day in 1869, after a long absence, he had returned to his native Catskill rivers "to pay my respects to them as an angler."

They struck the river quite unexpectedly in the middle of the afternoon at a point where it was a good-sized trout stream:

It proved to be one of those black mountain brooks born of innumerable ice-cold springs, nourished in the shade, and shod, as it were, with thick-matted moss, that every camper-out remembers. The fish are as black as the stream and very wild. They dart from beneath the fringed rocks, or dive with the hook into the dusky depths, an integral part of the silence and the shadows.

They crept upstream. The spell of the moss was over all, and with noiseless tread they leapt from stone to stone and from ledge to ledge along the bed of the stream:

"How cool it is!"

Burroughs looked up the dark, silent defile, heard the solitary voice of the water, and saw the decayed trunks of fallen trees bridging the stream. All he had dreamed as a boy, of the haunts of beasts of prey—the crouching feline tribes, especially at twilight with the gloom already deepening in the woods—came freshly to mind. They pressed on, wary and alert, speaking to each other in low tones.

Whether haunted or hallowed, the vaulted hemlock sanctuaries of this pristine stream were a place of reverence not only for itinerant anglers, but also for generations of Neversink natives. They made trouting their religion and could as easily fish while they worshipped as they could worship while fishing. This was borne out by one Claryville resident, Andrew Lang, who in 1894 confessed his Sunday weakness: "When I cannot keep the run of the sermon, I occupy myself by catching, in my imagination, large and lusty trout." And who could blame him, when on the church steeple, over his very head, was a weather vane in the image of an enormous trout?

The male population of Claryville were noted fishermen in those days. As soon as a boy got out of his cradle, he got into a trout brook; and by the time he arrived at the dignity of trousers, he knew more about catching trout than the city angler learned in a lifetime. It is told that, in the district schools, examinations on stream formation, location of pools, spring holes, and the like were regularly held, as well as trials of fly casting, and that the first problem in arithmetic began:

"If John has three trout and James has two, how many does the Yorker have?" The answer, of course, was "none."

For some men the Neversink was like a mistress. Its intimate beauty and seductive charm could overwhelm the beholder with an irresistible urge to possess, whether it took the form of outright ownership or just a little overnight poaching. One such man was Clarence Roof, New York importer of spaghetti and olive oil.

Roof came up regularly in the 1870s to the West Branch of the Neversink. He stayed at the "Parker Place," a small, informal hunting and fishing preserve. The proprietor, Martin Parker, was the first to stock and post this stream, but the local habitués ignored his signs and continued to fish it at will. Parker resisted, but the preserve was "poached by night and by day, the guardians were ill-treated and every effort was made to drive the members away or make their stay uncomfortable." Parker became discouraged and gave up, but not Roof. Infuriated, he wanted the poachers punished, and even more than that, he wanted the stream for himself. So he made Parker an offer he could not refuse. With the Parker Place as his centerpiece, Roof continued to buy surrounding farms until he had put together four thousand acres and five miles of trout stream. In one of the deeds he acquired, a former Indian owner had made a sign translated by a witness as "Wintoon." Roof liked the word so much that he chose it for the name of his Neversink preserve.

Under its new ownership, the West Branch of the Neversink became the setting for what the *Pine Hill Sentinel* billed as "The Great Trout Wars." It was Roof against the poachers, and he went after them with a vengeance. He had trespassers arrested and brought to court. He hired numerous lawyers to prosecute his cases. He pursued three young men for eight years through a series of trials and appeals, only to see them acquitted. But overall he succeeded in his goal to create a private preserve for himself, his friends, and his descendants. The river has been in the family for more than one hundred years.

Raphael Govin, one of Roof's lawyers from New York, shuttled back and forth from the city so often that he too fell in love with the

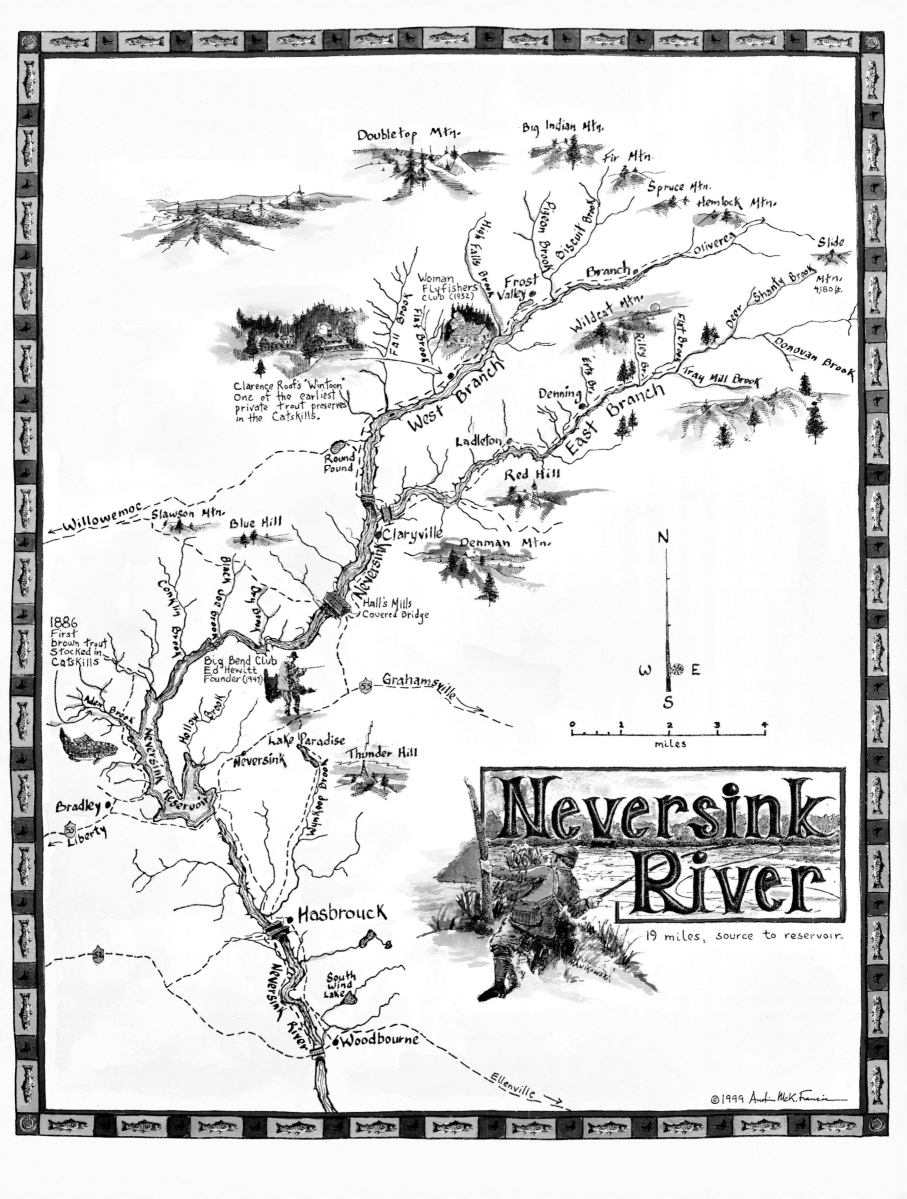

Doubletop Mtn.

Big Indian Mtn.

Fir Mtn.

Spruce Mtn.

Hemlock Mtn.

High Falls Brook

Pigeon Brook

Biscuit Brook

Oliverea

Branch

Slide Mtn. 4,180 ft.

Fall Brook

Flat Brook

Woman Flyfishers Club (1932)

Frost Valley

Wildcat Mtn.

Deer Shanty Brook

Flat Brook

Donovan Brook

West Branch

Clarence Roof's 'Wintoon' One of the earliest private trout preserves in the Catskills.

Denning

East Fork

Riley Br.

East Branch

Tray Mill Brook

Ladleton

Round Pound

Red Hill

Willowemoc

Slawson Mtn.

Blue Hill

Claryville

Denman Mtn.

N

Neversink

Conklin Brook

Black Joe Brook

Dry Brook

Hall's Mills Covered Bridge

W E

S

0 1 2 3 4
miles

1886 First brown trout Stocked in Catskills

Big Bend Club Ed Hewitt Founder (1941)

Grahamsville 55

Alex Brook

Hollow Brook

Neversink Reservoir

Lake Paradise

Neversink

Wynkoop Brook

Thunder Hill

Bradley

55 Liberty

Neversink River

19 miles, source to reservoir.

Hasbrouck

52

South Wind Lake

HANKOWSKI

Woodbourne

Ellenville →

Neversink River

©1999 Austin McK. Francis

*Looking downstream from the upper
end of Hall's Mills Bridge Pool.*

Neversink. With Roof's help, Govin was able to buy several thousand acres of his own, including five miles of the East Branch, the last mile downstream on the West Branch, and Round Pond, which he renamed Govin Lake.

Govin took a different approach to protecting his section of the river. Perhaps he rejected a "total lockout" policy because an old woman in the middle of his new estate refused to sell, or he may simply have wanted not to be a prosecutor both on and off the job. Whatever his reason, he chose to hire Ira Irwin, the valley's best-known poacher, as the caretaker of his property, and to post only certain stretches of the stream. As a result, Govin had far less trouble with poachers than Roof.

For all their efforts to acquire the streams, neither of these men was a dedicated fly fisherman. Roof preferred riding horseback around Wintoon, and Govin's only fishing was in his lake. He liked to be rowed around so he could troll for pickerel. The serious fly fishing at the time was being done a few miles farther downstream, on the main branch of the river, by a newcomer named Theodore Gordon.

Gordon moved to the Neversink in the early 1890s. It was there over the next twenty-five years that his fishing, writing, and flytying established him as the leading American angler of his day.

Gordon was a frail man, about five feet, three inches tall, weighing ninety pounds, and a consumptive. These qualities undoubtedly influenced his choice of a solitary life and helped him, as John McDonald observed, "to put one thing only into his mind—the stream—and sustain it there unflaggingly for a great many years."

He was also a lonely man, finding comfort in the tranquil muse of his fishing articles:

It is a bitter cold winter's night and I am far away from the cheerful lights of town or city. The north wind is shrieking and tearing at this lonely house, like some evil demon . . . the wood-burning stove is my only companion. It is on nights such as these that our thoughts stray to the time of leaf and blossom when birds sing merrily and trout are rising in the pools. Spring is near, quite near, and it will soon be time to go fishing. We want to talk about it dreadfully. O for a brother crank of the fly-fishing fraternity, one who would be ready to listen occasionally and not insist upon doing all the talking, telling all the stories himself. But if we cannot talk we can write, and it is just possible that some dear brother angler will read what we say upon paper. There is some comfort in that idea, so here goes.

Gordon tried in the winter to break up his daily routine to avoid boredom but admitted that one day was much like another. "What victims of habit we become," he said. "I write for two hours, tramp in the country two hours, lunch, tie flies, tramp again, and read all evening."

(Above) The middle of three of Ed Hewitt's log-and-plank dams left after the Neversink Reservoir flooded the lower water of his Big Bend Club; floods or ice have claimed them all, returning the river to its pre-Hewitt days.
Photograph by Linda Morgens.

(Right) Looking downstream at the narrow outlet of the Big Bend Pool, in fall low water; many of Hewitt's five-pounders lay in the eight-to-ten-foot depths along the rocky ledge between the two hemlocks.

In the spring, Gordon made trips to other Catskill rivers from his base on the Neversink, often staying a week or two at each one. On the Beaverkill he was welcome on the water of the Brooklyn Fly Fishers and up at J. L. Snedecor's stretch near Jones Falls. His stooped profile and long rod bobbing along the streams were a familiar sight on the Neversink, Willowemoc, and Beaverkill.

Gordon never owned property in the Catskills, and he never joined a fishing club. In a March 5, 1904, article in the *Fishing Gazette,* he wrote, "Our little club, the Fly Fishers, held its annual dinner at the Union League on February 6th." Until recently, all attempts to identify the club he referred to had failed. In Ed Van Put's research for his book *The Beaverkill,* he found an article in the *Roscoe-Rockland Review* that pinned down Gordon's attendance on that same night *as an invited guest* at the eighth annual meeting and dinner of the Fly Fishers Club of Brooklyn. With a standing invitation to fish the Brooklyn water, Gordon obviously felt as much a member as his hosts.

Although he fished private water, and had many invitations to do so because of his fame, Gordon was philosophically disposed to public fishing. "Hard-fished, free water is a better test than a preserve where there are but a few fishers," he said, "but one must be liberal-minded enough to allow every mon to gang his ain gait and think and fish as he wishes."

In 1918, three years after Gordon's death, Edward Ringwood Hewitt arrived on the Neversink to fill the vacuum. And if any man had the presence and self-esteem to think he could do so, certainly that man was Hewitt. The happy outcome was that he made just as valuable a contribution to angling as Gordon did, but in a marvelously different way.

Ed Hewitt was born into "good solid old New York money"—his grandfather Peter Cooper built the first steam locomotive in America—and was educated as a graduate chemist. He also had the natural talent of a mechanical engineer. Over his lifetime he was granted dozens of patents for a wide variety of inventions, including a black-fly deterrent, the felt-soled wading shoe, an opaque fishing leader, a fishing-line grease, a silent shotgun cartridge, a soap calculated to keep your hands warm in cold water, the bivisible fly (one both he and the fish could see), and a fishing reel that would come apart with the removal of one screw.

Given his abilities, his wealth, and a deep love for trout fishing, it was almost foreordained that Hewitt should become the greatest experimenter in the history of fly fishing. And his laboratory was to be the same section of the Neversink that Gordon lived next to and fished so often. In fact, before Gordon died, Hewitt and LaBranche used to drive up to fish Clarence Roof's water and have dinner with Gordon on the way home. Sparse Grey Hackle, in a letter to Harry Darbee, said, "Bub, what would you give to have been a fly on the wall at those sessions?"

In 1918, Hewitt began accumulating twenty-seven hundred acres and four miles of river between the village of Neversink and Hall's Mills Bridge. Herman Christian sold Hewitt the river frontage that included the Big Bend pool, having bought it as

Hewitt's secret agent only days earlier. On his new property, Hewitt enthusiastically set out on the twin projects of scientific trout raising and stream improvement. Some of his experiments were quite ambitious. He imported salmon eggs from Norway to see if they could be established in the Neversink. He tried to increase the variety and quantity of trout food by bringing over nymphs and larvae of English stream insects. And in his waning years, as a ninety year old, when most men would have been vegetating, he sponsored an elaborate three-year project to bring impregnated Atlantic salmon eggs over from Scotland, hatch them, and plant the unfed fry in the river.

About 1933 Hewitt began to feel the effects of the Depression. "He'd lost a great deal of money, which he'd made from his inventions," said Mabel Ingalls. "He needed to run his mind to other ways of making money, so he decided to rent out rods on his part of the Neversink." About thirty anglers took advantage of the privilege for $120 a year; they became known as the Neversink Rods, with headquarters in an old farmhouse located on high ground overlooking the river at the lower end of the property. It was an inspired answer to Hewitt's dilemma, for it not only paid for his experiments but also gave him a way of testing their effectiveness.

When his rods were in attendance, Hewitt spent his time showing them how to fish, making sure that any large fish they caught got released, and driving everyone around in an antique high-sprung sedan whose canvas top was aluminum-painted to reflect heat. A hole was pierced at the rear to serve as a rod holder. His rods called this vehicle the "mechanical goat," and he took them anywhere and everywhere in it at terrifying speeds.

Edward R. Hewitt (left) and George M. L. LaBranche (below) in the etchings of Gordon Stevenson.
Courtesy Anglers' Club of New York.

When he was about eighty, Hewitt decided to change his Neversink camp from one with a yearly rod-rental basis to a fishing club for half a dozen or so permanent members. Contributing to his decision was the lower level of rod rentals that started during the car-and-gas shortage of World War II and persisted after the war was over. Another major influence was the imminent loss of over half of his river mileage to the Neversink Reservoir, which had been blocked out by New York City and was resuming construction after the war.

One of the benefits to Hewitt from this new arrangement was that he could turn the upkeep of his property over to the club members and continue to fish and pursue such experiments as importing salmon eggs, at the same time creating a self-supporting place of summer recreation for his descendants. Thus was born the Big Bend Club, which continues to this day.

Hewitt's Neversink experiences were the foundation and substance of several books on angling: *Telling on the Trout* (1926), *Hewitt's*

(Above) This ghostly image, from an old home movie, is of the Hewitt camp once located overlooking the Neversink River at a point now buried beneath the waters of the reservoir.
Courtesy Anglers' Club of New York.

(Right) Colonel Ambrose Monell and George LaBranche, standing on Monell's Neversink Gorge stoop, fronting the stretch of river assembled by Ed Hewitt for Monell when he said how much he admired Hewitt's water several miles upstream.
Courtesy Harry Rhulen.

*A gentler stretch of the Neversink Gorge,
above Denton Falls.*

The Neversink in early October below the reservoir; low-water fishing to a baetis hatch, more to be out there at a pretty time than to catch fish.

Photograph by Richard Franklin.

Handbook of Fly Fishing (1933), *Nymph Fly Fishing* (1934), and *Seventy-Five Years a Fisherman for Salmon and Trout* (1948).

Besides his trout studies and books, Hewitt was also a consultant "on fishery matters for a large number of clients." Solving their problems added to a fund of experience that he felt was so much greater than anyone else's that he claimed: "I expect I know more about trout than anyone else in the country."

In an interview shortly before his death in 1957, Hewitt said that he wanted to have his ashes thrown into the Neversink. "That way," he said, "it will give the trout a chance to get even."

Artist Mead Schaeffer, one of Ed Hewitt's "rods," at Hewitt's camp, taken about 1948 by Leslie Gill.
Courtesy Frances McLaughlin-Gill.

The waxy petals, fallen in the pool,
Made the black water with their beauty gay;
Here might the redbird come his plumes to cool,
And court the flower that cheapens his array.
—JOSHUA GEROW

SIX

Esopus Creek

~~~~~~

The Esopus is the most hospitable of the Catskill rivers. Some who know its often muddy and turbulent waters may wonder why. Simply, the Esopus welcomes all comers.

It was home to the Algonquin tribe, who chose its gentler valley over those of the Beaverkill, Willowemoc, and Neversink, into all of which they traveled to hunt. The name Esopus was first given to the stream by the Dutch settlers. It was their version of the Algonquin word for "small brook." The name was so successful—perhaps because it sounds so nearly like a stream itself—that Esopus became the name also of the Indian tribe and then of all the land in the valley.

As the most accessible Catskill river from New York City, Esopus Creek was among the first to open its doors to visiting fishermen. In 1830, as sport fishing was just beginning to catch on in this country, the Esopus already had a boardinghouse, run by Milo Barber in Shandaken, which catered to anglers from the city.

The nearness of Kingston on the Hudson River played a large role in the early development of Esopus Creek as a favorite of trout fishermen. To reach the Esopus in the mid-1800s, a fisherman boarded a steamboat in Manhattan and changed to a stagecoach at Kingston for the twenty- or thirty-mile trip to the villages along the river.

When railroads came into the Catskills, it was a Hudson River steamboat company, Romer & Tremper, that took advantage of its ready-made market and in 1879 opened the first "railroad hotel" on the Esopus. Everything must have been up for grabs: the steamboat crowd installed Major Jacob H. Tremper as manager of the new Tremper House and had the name of the town changed to Mount Tremper and the mountain behind the hotel renamed Tremper Mountain. To keep things in balance, an opposing peak on the other side of the river was given the name Romer Mountain.

Tremper House had many novel attractions as a resort hotel, including

Elmer's Bend, on the Esopus below Phoenicia.

85

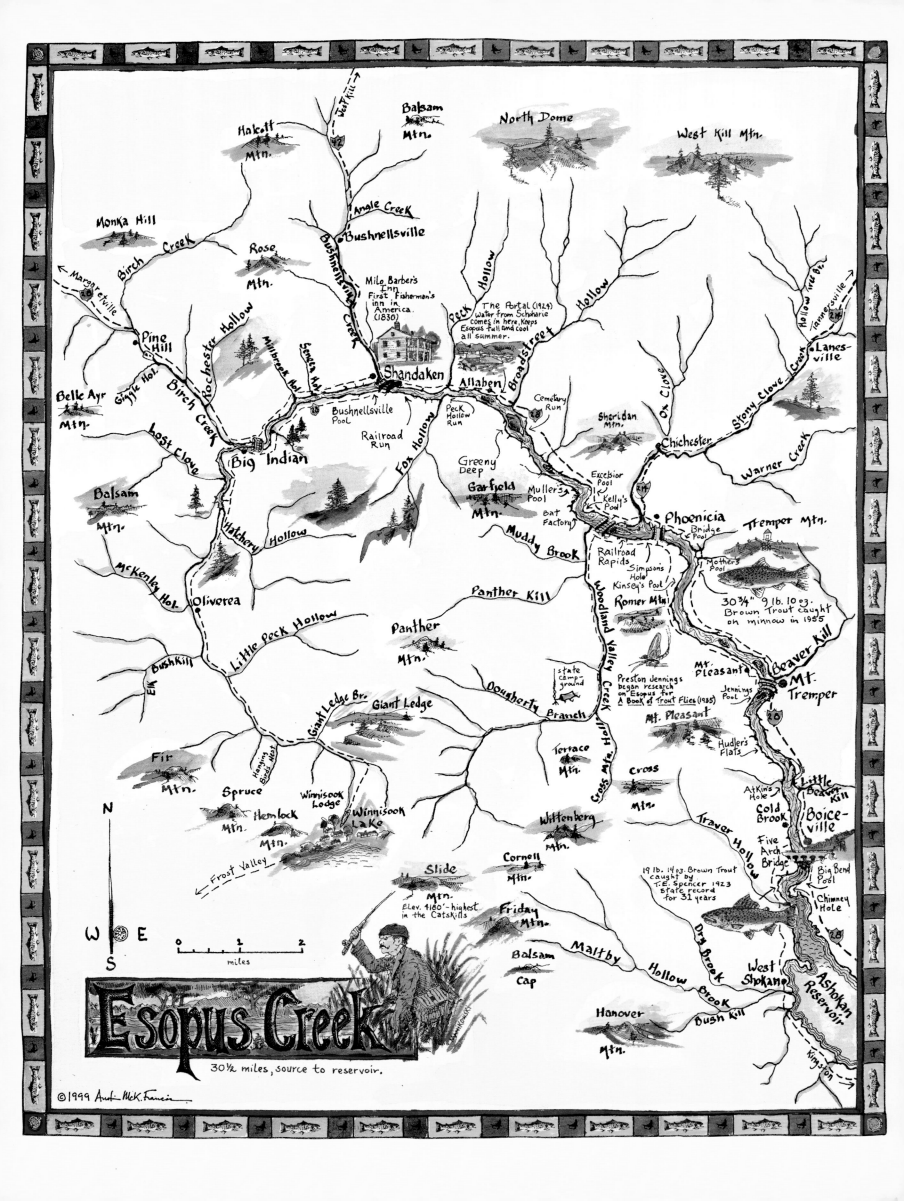

Esopus Creek

30½ miles, source to reservoir.

© 1999 Austin McK. Francis

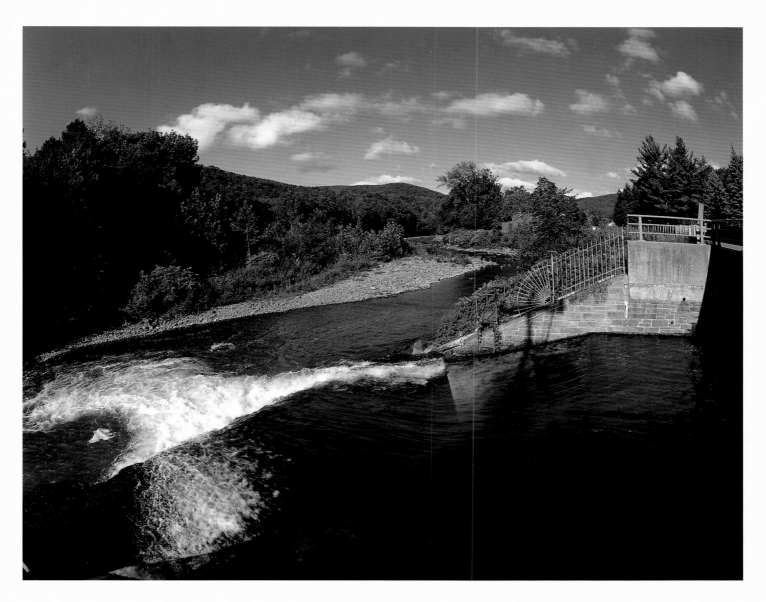

From this tunnel—known as "the Portal"—up to 600 million gallons a day of Schoharie Reservoir water are emptied into the Esopus, having both good and bad effects on the fishing. When it runs heavily, the river discolors and becomes dangerous to wade. On the positive side, the portal sustains the river with cool, full flows at times when other streams are warm and low.

elevators, steam heat, bathrooms, and even a resident physician. Dr. H.R. Winter was an ardent fisherman "who often prescribed a course of trout fishing for businessmen wearied in the pursuit of dollars . . . and he was as ready with advice on trout flies and rods as he was with pills and powders."

Beyond Mount Tremper, the Ulster & Delaware trains made stops along the Esopus at Phoenicia, Shandaken, and Big Indian. It was so convenient that a fisherman could practically get on the train in his waders and pile right off into his favorite pool.

Happily for anglers, the Esopus extended its hospitality to the rainbow trout. Although there are large wild rainbows in the Delaware, and stories of bygone runs of rainbows up the Willowemoc, Esopus Creek is the only Catskill river in which rainbows have thrived since they were imported from California in the late 1800s.

Theodore Gordon told a story about the Esopus rainbows that had been seen in the spring of 1902 jumping below Bishop's Falls, now covered by the Ashokan Reservoir:

Precipitous walls of rock rise on both sides of the deep pool below these falls, the formation resembling a western canyon, and as no boat was available it seemed impossible to reach the fish. A mill is perched upon the cliff above the pool, and the miller conceived a brilliant plan of action. He baited a good-sized hook with a large hellgrammite and lowered it from the window of his mill, down, down into the foam and spray far below. He struck a fish at once, and actually succeeded in hauling or reeling it up into the room in which he stood. It proved to be a fine specimen of the rainbow trout ("Salmo irideus"), eighteen inches long. I have not visited these falls for two years, but think the distance between the water and the window must have been about fifty feet. Lucky miller!

In 1906, before the Ashokan Reservoir or Shandaken Tunnel were built on the Esopus, Gordon observed in one of his *Forest and Stream* articles, "It is the only stream I know of where rainbow trout actually remained and multiplied for many years." He also noted in the same article that if you stocked Catskill streams with rainbows, "they might go to sea in the second year, but that is the risk one would have to run."

As if in answer to Gordon, the very next year New York City began building the Ashokan Reservoir, the first in its Catskill water-supply system, and when it was finished in 1915, the rainbows of the Esopus had their own little private ocean to run down to, feed, and grow in.

The Esopus was to have one more major physical change in order to provide New York City with water. In 1917, work started on Schoharie Reservoir, one valley to the north. To channel its water most efficiently into the supply system, the city hit upon an ingenious idea. It was customary to build an underground tunnel connecting two reservoirs; but someone noticed that Esopus Creek was directly in line between the Schoharie and

Larry Decker, Goshen, New York, holding his 30½-inch, nine-pound, ten-ounce brown trout in front of Blanche and Dick Kahil's Rainbow Lodge. Situation: early spring of 1955, heavy water, fly rod and automatic reel, two minnows with lots of weight, trout hits them just behind a big rock in Mother's Pool.

Photograph by Ed Pfizenmaier.

Ashokan reservoirs, and the Shandaken Tunnel idea was born. By running the tunnel only two-thirds of the way, surfacing at Allaben, and using the Esopus riverbed to carry Schoharie water the rest of the way to the Ashokan, approximately ten miles of burrowing and construction were saved.

On February 9, 1924, the first water was sent through Shandaken Tunnel, twenty-six-hundred feet beneath Balsam Mountain, and Esopus Creek became a unique trout river, certainly in the Catskills, if not in the entire country.

More remarkable than its man-made uniqueness, the Esopus conceals beneath its topography the remains of a suspected cataclysmic event that occurred nearly 400 million years ago and would lead to the creation of a river whose shape and flow are unlike any other in the Catskills. Viewed from a point directly above Panther Mountain, the Esopus headwaters and its main tributary, Woodland Creek, form a perfect circle six miles in diameter with Panther's peak in the center.

About 1976, New York geologist Yngvar Isachsen—after disproving

The Phoenicia Hotel, opened in 1854, was the setting for Anglers' Club of New York outings in the 1920s. They had such good times that one member wrote an article in the club bulletin describing the hotel as the "Matawan of the Esopus." Matawan was a mental hospital in eastern New Jersey.

more likely explanations such as subsurface salt domes and granite masses—demonstrated that the probable cause of this unusual river shape was the impact of an asteroid. As large as a half-mile across, the asteroid approached from the south and gouged out the crater whose rim is now the river's course. Subsequent ocean-borne sediments, bedrock impactions, upheavals, and erosions created the Esopus we know today.

*   *   *

The Phoenicia Hotel was a popular hangout for angling notables in the 1920s. The Anglers' Club of New York held its "Annual Outing and Trout

Excelsior Pool, upstream from Phoenicia.

Fishing Championship" there in 1922, and its members often gathered there to fish and relax. They had such good times that one of the members felt disposed to write a pen-named article in the club bulletin describing the various ways members disported themselves on and off the stream. In it he referred to the Phoenicia Hotel as the "Matawan of the Esopus." Matawan was a well-appointed mental institution in eastern New Jersey where acquaintances could sometimes be found if they let the market get too much with them.

Even without the self-inflicted distractions of its fishermen, the Esopus on its own power has always been a maddening trout stream. Its regulars can frequently be heard to say they love and hate it in the same breath. Almost without exception this frustration comes from the fact that the fisherman is often fishing in cloudy to downright muddy water. Deposits of fine-grained red clay peculiar to the Esopus and Schoharie drainages cause a lot of this "turbidity," a name preferred by the state's Department of Environmental

Rainbow Run, on the Esopus at Mount Tremper.

Rock Cut, looking downstream from the Route 28 bridge at Mount Tremper. Big-fish anglers have taken a lot of large trout out of the very deep hole here.

Conservation, which, if it bestows an air of institutional resignation or inevitability to the condition, is most apt.

Any good rainstorm can force one of the Esopus's tributaries into a clay bank, and it will run discolored for a year or more until that clay deposit is gone. One can go up the tributary and find exactly where the clay is, and above it the water will be clear. A deposit as small as a wheelbarrow can discolor the entire stream.

Shandaken Tunnel is the other main source of Esopus turbidity. It has come to be known as "the Portal," connoting not so much a conduit from another watershed as a giant mouth that disgorges millions of gallons a day (mgd's) of water into the stream. Portal water is filled with silt and increases in opacity as the six-hundred-mgd capacity of the tunnel is approached. It is believed that the source of the silt is a combination of a sediment layer on the bottom of Schoharie Reservoir, over ten feet thick near the intake gates of the tunnel, and the lining of the tunnel itself.

The Portal has a tremendous impact on the Esopus. On the negative side, it adds to the discoloring problem already present in nature, and its heavier releases create dangerous wading conditions.

Positively, the Portal sustains the river with cool, full flows at times when other streams are warm and low. In midsummer, up to 90 percent of the flow below the Portal is Schoharie water. And, best of all, mixed in with the inorganic silt from Schoharie Reservoir is a rich profusion of daphnia—tiny transparent water fleas—on which the native rainbows gorge and thrive. One other benefit is the presence of large walleyes that come through the tunnel and settle in the Portal pool. It is no wonder that this pool is a favorite of bait fishermen.

From the time Shandaken Tunnel was completed, New York City water officials decided how the Portal would run based on criteria oriented exclusively to the city's water requirements. Sometimes it would run "full pipe," causing the lower Esopus to roar down its course, discouraging any attempts to fish even with bait. Sometimes, immediately afterward, it would be shut off completely, leaving the river slack and the fish scurrying to get back into the main channel. This went on for more than fifty years.

Then, in 1974, two major fish kills occurred on the Esopus, and the fishermen were galvanized into action. In January and again in October, the Portal got shut down abruptly, leaving thousands of trout and lesser fish stranded in the side channels of the river. Trout Unlimited and Theodore Gordon Flyfishers had already been fighting for improved release patterns, and now there arose a new group to lead the troops into battle. Frank Mele of Woodstock, New York, organized a coalition of anglers and friendly parties called Catskill Waters, whose mission was to

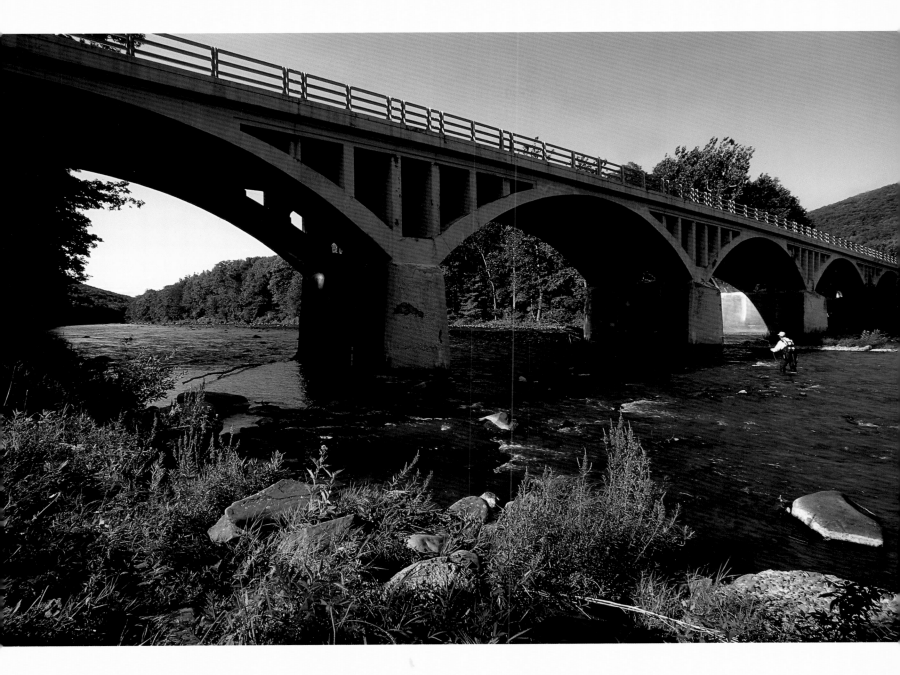

Five Arch Bridge, a river landmark and favorite fishing spot of many Esopus anglers. It was from behind one of these piers after a heavy November rainstorm that Arnold Gingrich got snatched by the current and rolled downstream end over end until he wound up "plastered against a large rock like Shakespeare's 'alligarter on a wall.'"

lobby for state legislation to balance the erratic reservoir releases affecting about 180 miles of prime trout water. Catskill Waters was officially launched in January 1975, with John Hoeko of Fleischmanns, New York, as its president and chief lobbyist in Albany. Financial support came from members of TU, TGF, and the Federation of Fly Fishermen, as well as from sympathetic individuals. Ogden Reid, DEC commissioner, convinced by Mele and Hoeko of the situation's urgency, backed their efforts and steered them to the state attorney general's office, whose staff offered advice and technical assistance in drafting an amendment to the conservation law.

In the summer of 1976, after many months of intensive lobbying efforts, and strong opposition by New York City, Title 8 of Article 15 of the Environmental Conservation Law passed in the New York Assembly by nineteen votes and in the Senate by a single vote, and, after a last-moment veto threat, was signed into law on July 28 by Governor Hugh Carey.

This law empowered the DEC to orchestrate reservoir releases, but not to change the aggregate amount of water flowing from the dams. This was fixed by a Supreme Court decree. In effect, the DEC was given "first hand" on the valve.

Rules were drawn, based on this enabling legislation, to govern the opening and closing of the intake gates at the Schoharie end of Shandaken Tunnel. However, although New York City is bound by the rules to cooperate with the DEC, the rules are binding only five months a year (June 1st to October 31st) and indeed are inoperative if their observance should cause a loss of water over the spillways of either the Gilboa (Schoharie) or the Ashokan dam.

Nevertheless, since the new release rules took effect in June of 1977, there have been pronounced improvements in the temperatures and water levels of the lower Esopus. A July 1978 survey, in which temperatures were taken every day, showed that the water below the Portal averaged more than 13 degrees cooler than above. Even as it flowed past the Cold Brook gauging station, eleven miles farther downstream, it was averaging 4 degrees cooler. And, instead of finding the river at flood stage one day and in drought conditions the next, rarely—because of the operation of the Portal—is the river too high or too low. As a result, setting out to fish the Esopus is no longer the risky venture it used to be. Stream management has become a reality.

Even more significant than the improvements to Esopus fishing was the precedent that had been set. For the first time since 1907, when it annexed the Catskills into its water supply system, New York City had made a formal accommodation to the rivers affected by its dams. Many unsuccessful attempts had been made in the past to gain "conservation releases" from the three dams on the East and West branches of the Delaware and the Neversink. The situation on those rivers was far more complex, though, with several states involved and a federal river master in Montague, New Jersey. Thus it was harder to postulate the negative effects of curtailed flows and the benefits of conservation releases.

"But here it was dramatic," said one of the Esopus regulars, "with the extreme flows from the Portal and the fish dying all over the place. That was what allowed us to get our hands on the city." And that was what paved the way for a series of release agreements for the other reservoirs that substantially improved many miles of Catskill trout fishing.

Chimney Hole, the last pool before Esopus Creek enters the Ashokan Reservoir. It was here in 1923 that T. E. Spencer caught a nineteen-pound, fourteen-ounce brown trout, a state record for thirty-one years.

SEVEN

Schoharie Creek

The crew from Westkill Tavern had quit fishing for the day, and, heading back upriver, they stopped at Billy Boyd's. He was sitting in the back room, overlooking the stream, surrounded by his cats. The boardinghouse, long since out of business, was now occupied only by eighty-year-old Billy, and as he sat there, bats flew in and out of the screenless windows, picking off the evening's hatch as it circled above him around a bare bulb. Pointing to his attic, Billy grinned and said, "I keep bats up there!"

That was back in the early forties, when the bass were so plentiful in Schoharie Creek that a special regulation favoring trout was passed allowing fishermen to keep as many bass as they could catch, regardless of size. And Billy Boyd was cut out for the job. Camped there next to one of the best pools on the whole river, he loved to catch bass, and his cats loved to eat them. His only problem was getting flies, and for that he had a novel solution.

Art Flick, proprietor of Westkill Tavern, always warned his guests to be on guard against Billy. But he was so full of himself and of stories and charm that they fell to him every time.

"Gosh, fellows, those bass are pretty bad out there, but I guess I don't have to tell *you* how they bother your flies," Billy would say.

"They sure are, Billy," one of his visitors would answer. "I wish we could do something about it."

"Well, I'd get quite a few of them," he would say, opening up one of those little blue Edgeworth tobacco tins with a single, well-chewed bucktail in it, "but I've just got this one fly."

At that point the guys from the tavern would fight with one another over the privilege of giving Billy some flies. As Art recalled: "George Newman, one of them who should have known better, said, 'Billy, we'll just take care of that.' And he runs up to his car, gets his big tackle box, comes down, opens it up, and says, 'Billy, help yourself!' And, of course,

Ledgerock Pool above Bay Bridge on the West Kill, tributary of Schoharie Creek, the beginning of a series of deep undercut banks, ledgerock, and freestone pools all the way up into Spruceton.

Westkill Tavern, which Art Flick took over from his parents in 1934 as a country inn catering to trout fishermen and grouse hunters. Many well-known anglers, including Ray Bergman and Preston Jennings, considered this a favorite base of operations. In 1960, Flick sold Westkill Tavern and retired from innkeeping; three years later it was destroyed by fire.
Courtesy the Flick family.

Art Flick and Billy Boyd teamed up to cut back the excessive numbers of black bass in the Schoharie. Flick lobbied successfully for a no-limit regulation for Schoharie bass only, and Boyd took advantage of it by catching thousands of them out of the pool behind his house. Schoharie trout fishing improved dramatically as a result.
Courtesy the Flick family.

the old man always obliged them. I think he had more flies than all of our guests put together."

Bass were not always so bothersome to Schoharie trout fishermen. The problem started when Gilboa Dam was completed in 1926 and the waters of the reservoir rose to cover Devasego Falls, a forty-foot-high barrier to the fish of the lower river. A mile and a half downriver from Prattsville, the falls before then had divided the fishing into pike and bass water below and trout water above.

In a 1934 biological survey by New York State of the Schoharie watershed, it was noted that Gilboa Dam "has been responsible for the introduction of small-mouthed bass in the upper Schoharie, thereby doing great harm to the trout fishing. The bass have become very numerous in the section above the reservoir, having run upstream as far as Hunter." As one fisherman of that day put it, "The bass were just swarming up in this stream. After the water got up to fifty degrees you simply couldn't catch a trout. The bass were so thick in there that no matter what you threw in, even almost a bare hook, you got a bass."

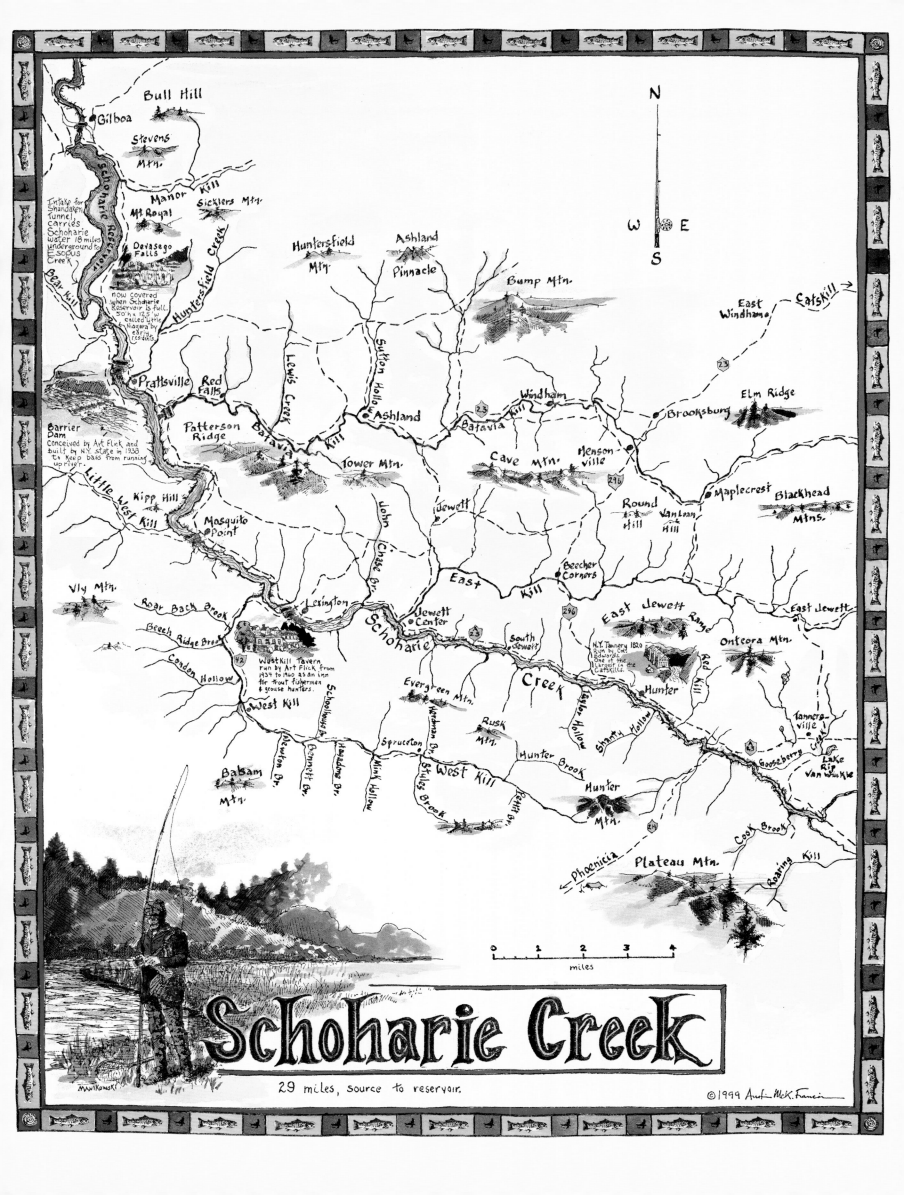

Schoharie Creek

29 miles, source to reservoir.

©1999 Austin McK. Francis

(Above) A small V-dam and plunge pool on the upper Spruceton section of the West Kill, three miles above which the stream begins on Hunter Mountain.

(Above left) The old Electric Light Dam, above Hunter on the Schoharie, formerly a privately owned power-generating dam, good holding water for wild rainbows and brook trout.

(Below left) The Shadows, last pool on the Schoharie before the West Kill joins it.

That was the Schoharie in 1934, when Art Flick arrived fresh from New York City with his wife and two young sons. Leaving his job as manager of a Kinney shoe store, he took over the Westkill Tavern from his parents, who had run it as an ordinary resort hotel since the early 1920s. His hope was to pursue a lifelong interest in fishing and hunting and turn the Westkill Tavern into a first-class establishment catering to trout fishermen and grouse hunters.

A major factor in Art's decision to become a professional innkeeper and outdoorsman was the Anglers' Club of New York's selection that year of Westkill Tavern as headquarters for its fourteenth Annual Outing and Trout Fishing Championship. Apparently, Ray Bergman's glowing reports of his visits in Westkill and of the local rivers had persuaded the Anglers' Club to come to the Schoharie for the first time, breaking a six-year string of outings at DeBruce Club Inn on the Willowemoc.

Only after being so auspiciously launched did Art find out about the bass problem. "Had I known, I don't think I would have had guts enough to come into it," he said. But he *was* in it, and there was no way out except to fight the bass. In doing that, Art began a personal commitment to Schoharie Creek that lasted for over fifty years.

Ladyes Bridge Pool on the West Kill.
*The valley ran below me, disappearing
behind mountain shoulders, reappearing
where the brook had widened its tenure in
the course of centuries. Southward rose the
Big Westkill, stern in its own shadow, and
still topped with cloud.* —T. MORRIS
LONGSTRETH

Over those years, the Schoharie benefited from Art Flick's commitment in many ways. There was the barrier dam at Prattsville to keep more bass from running upstream, which he conceived and pushed through with the help of the Conservation Department. The state's condition was that Art find donors of land on opposite sides of the stream suitable for locating the dam. This he did, and the diplomatic effort it required soon spun off into one of New York's first public fishing rights acquisition programs. Shortly after the barrier dam was completed in 1938, Art lobbied successfully for the special bass-fishing regulation on which Billy Boyd and his cats thrived. In the first week after the new regulation took effect, more than 1,000 bass were taken by hook and line above the barrier dam. Gradually, the bass population dwindled in the upper river, and word got around that Schoharie trout fishing had improved tremendously. Art's fishing log bore this out: over the fourteen years following the dam's installation, he averaged over forty-five days on the stream each year and over 13 trout per day, for a total of 8,648 trout.

Besides the barrier dam, there were the willows Art and his sons planted each year with seedlings provided by the state, mostly along the West Kill, his home tributary of the Schoharie. There always seemed to be a new stretch of raw, begravelled bank in need of the holding power of the willows' water-seeking roots. They are planted simply by anchoring them with rocks on the bottom in about six inches of water, so that when the stream goes down, the roots will still have moisture. Once they are established, it is next to impossible to wash them out. Not only do they hold the bank, they also harbor trout among their roots and dress up an otherwise barren stream border.

And then there was the Westkill Tavern itself. Art thought of it and ran it as a private club. In its later years he even renamed it Westkill Tavern Club. To be a "member" you had to meet Art's personal standards as a proper sportsman, which meant that you fly-fished or hunted grouse. Non-sporting guests were taken in as long as they were spoken for by a sportsman.

Fishermen staying at Westkill Tavern were encouraged to put back all fish under twelve inches, keeping the smaller ones only on their last day if they wanted to take some home to eat. "It was just something that I suggested," said Art. "They didn't have to do it. I was trying to keep fish in the stream, and it worked out quite well.

"As for our grouse hunters, I had them all trained to go and ask for permission. And for that

Boulder Run (opposite), Art Flick's favorite stretch of the Schoharie, and the plaque placed next to it by Trout Unlimited and friends to commemorate his pioneering role in stream entomology and the conservation of trout rivers.

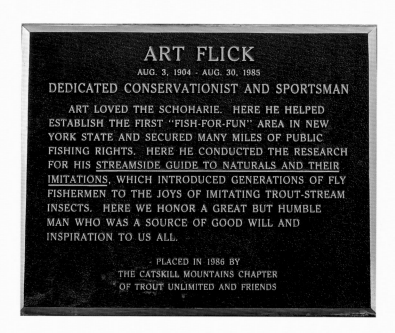

ART FLICK

AUG. 3, 1904 - AUG. 30, 1985

DEDICATED CONSERVATIONIST AND SPORTSMAN

ART LOVED THE SCHOHARIE. HERE HE HELPED
ESTABLISH THE FIRST "FISH-FOR-FUN" AREA IN NEW
YORK STATE AND SECURED MANY MILES OF PUBLIC
FISHING RIGHTS. HERE HE CONDUCTED THE RESEARCH
FOR HIS STREAMSIDE GUIDE TO NATURALS AND THEIR
IMITATIONS, WHICH INTRODUCED GENERATIONS OF FLY
FISHERMEN TO THE JOYS OF IMITATING TROUT-STREAM
INSECTS. HERE WE HONOR A GREAT BUT HUMBLE
MAN WHO WAS A SOURCE OF GOOD WILL AND
INSPIRATION TO US ALL.

· PLACED IN 1986 BY
THE CATSKILL MOUNTAINS CHAPTER
OF TROUT UNLIMITED AND FRIENDS

The barrier dam on Schoharie Creek at Prattsville, conceived and promoted by Art Flick, and built by the state in 1938. Its purpose—and it has been a huge success— is to keep bass from invading the river's upper reaches and competing with trout.

reason we had no trouble whatsoever with the landowners. There were very few places where our guests weren't welcome. I always stressed the point, 'When you go up to ask permission, tell them you are staying at the Westkill Tavern.' So that after a while the owners got a pretty good idea of the kind of people we had."

Ray Camp, outdoor columnist for the *New York Times*, was one of those people. He stayed at Westkill Tavern and fished the Schoharie regularly, and yet he never mentioned the river by name in his articles. Realizing that he could spoil a stream as fragile as the Schoharie, he always called it "West Kill" and he never exaggerated. Said Art, "He came up here so much he knew our people, many of them members of the Anglers' Club, and he knew darned well when he mentioned the West Kill, all the boys would realize he was talking about the Schoharie."

Chip Stauffer, a fly fisherman from Bucks County, Pennsylvania, who raised his own gamecock hackles, was another regular at the Westkill Tavern. One July day in 1934, he arrived with a newcomer named Preston Jennings, who was immersed in a project that would change Art Flick's life and make Schoharie Creek the setting for research that would enhance the fishing for thousands of eastern anglers.

Jennings was compiling the first American trout-stream entomology to give reliable identification of natural insects matched with the correct artificial fly and its dressing. He talked Art Flick into becoming one of his main bug collectors for *A Book of Trout Flies*. In the process Jennings introduced Flick to natural dun hackles and taught him the "difference between a good and bad fly." Persevering in his stream studies and fly-tying, Art eventually became an expert in his own right. He went down to speak at the Anglers' Club in New York, and his longtime friend Ray Camp began hounding him to write a book himself. Camp finally won when he called the Westkill Tavern from an Italian battlefront: "I want to know if you're going to do that book!"

The result, which came out in 1947, was *Art Flick's Streamside Guide to Naturals and Their Imitations*, and its distinguishing achievement was the substantial reduction of "must" patterns a fisherman had to have in his fly box. With its simplified emergence tables, identification system, and guide to selecting the "right fly"—based on Art Flick's Schoharie Creek research—this little book was "all the angler needed to know about trout-stream insects and their imitations." Since it was first published, *Streamside Guide* has sold over 150,000 copies.

Flick is gone, but his little book is still going strong. As for the Westkill Tavern, it came to a violent, fiery end in 1963, three years after Flick sold it and retired from innkeeping. Watching it burn just next door to his house, he said, "was like losing my own child."

EIGHT

Branches of the Delaware

~~~~~~~~~~~~~~~~~~~~~~~~~~~~~~~~~~~~~~~

Many years ago, there were arguments over where the Delaware River originated. "Some people denied that the Delaware has any true source at all," wrote Alf Evers in *The Catskills,* "but that it begins as a cooperative venture in which many streams share."

A likely pretender to the source is the Delaware's East Branch, whose headsprings seep out of the 2,400-foot-high flank of Irish Mountain near Grand Gorge. From there the river flows 330 miles—interrupted by Pepacton Reservoir—past Hancock, where it is joined by its sister, West Branch, then past Lordville, Hankins, Callicoon, swelling as it goes, past Cochecton, Port Jervis, and finally Pea Patch Island off Delaware City, into Delaware Bay.

A cold-water zone on the East Branch below Firemen's Field, not far downstream from Pepacton Dam. The angler here is fishing a riffle area with undercut banks on the left that hide wild fish, and where sulphurs hatch all summer long. Herons like it too.

The Pepacton Dam was completed in 1956 at Downsville on the East Branch. It created a narrow, twisting reservoir of some seven thousand acres, eliminating a little over twenty miles of river. This new reservoir took over court-mandated downstream releases from Neversink Reservoir. These releases came from the colder, bottom layer of the reservoir and were sufficient to establish a cold-water trout zone all the way past Hancock down to Long Eddy, a distance of some forty-five river miles.

The lower stretches of this new cold-water zone—they were below Ed Hewitt's "trout minimum" elevation of 1,000 feet—had always been more hospitable to warm-water species. So, as the trout began to establish

111

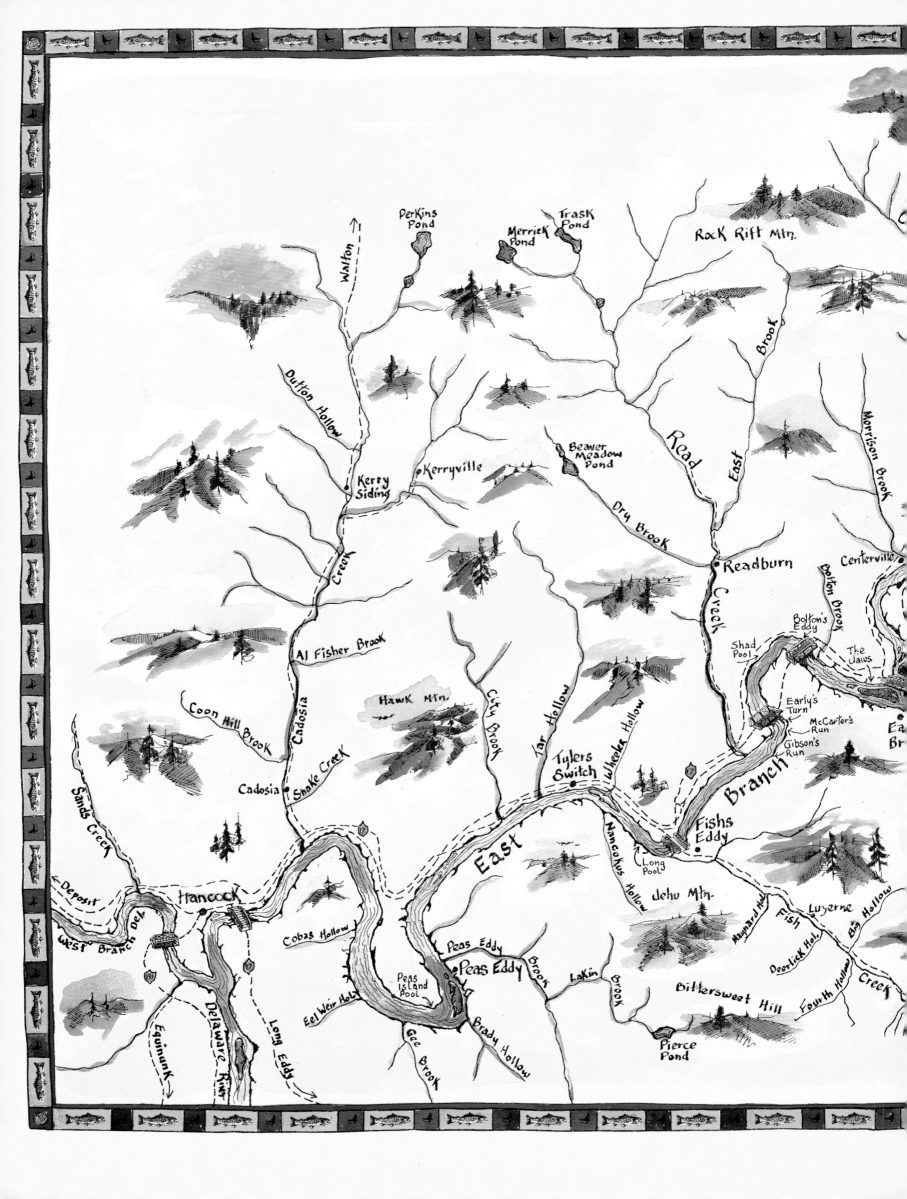

East Branch Delaware River

33 ½ miles, dam to junction with West Branch.

©1999 Austin McK. Francis

themselves lower down in the river, this new trout zone became
a favorite place for the local experts to fish. Harry Darbee, Sam
Hendrickson, Bill Kelly, Alan Fried, Joe Horak, and a select few of their
friends from the city all used to fish this stretch in the mid-sixties. It
had terrific hatches, good flow, cold water all the way down, and lots
of one- and two-pound fish.

The Pepacton-created trout zone lasted for about eleven years,
until the West Branch reservoir at Cannonsville came onstream in 1967
and once again the release patterns shifted. Because the West Branch is
subjected to greater pollution than the East Branch—it has many more
farms and towns in its valley—its water is considered more expendable
by New York City water managers. Thus the Cannonsville Reservoir
was given the brunt of the downstream release requirements.

And therein lies its unique character. With steady releases out of
the Cannonsville dam, the West Branch flows consistently cool and

full. By late July and August, the East Branch in its lower half becomes increasingly a smallmouth bass fishery. Its trout, seeking cooler water, move up closer to the Pepacton Dam or drop down into the main Delaware. It often happens that you can be fishing at the junction of the branches where the warm and cool flows meet and, depending on where you cast, catch trout on one side of the river and smallmouth on the other.

With the Pepacton and Cannonsville dams being thirty-three and eighteen miles up their respective branches, releases from the Cannonsville dam pushed the cold-water zone even farther down the main river to Callicoon. And there it remains today with some seasonal and legally allowable fluctuations. Other Delaware watershed dams have surfaced in the plans of water-thirsty minions, but they have stalled against political hurdles, public outcries, or technical impracticalities.

Nonetheless, what the dams have taken away in river miles they have given back in fishing benefits. In the dog-day weeks when other Catskill streams are flat and hot, the East and West branches flow steady and cool. A spring-creek environment—with lots of aquatic weeds loaded with little freshwater shrimp and a rich variety of insects—gives trout a longer growing season. All this equals more and bigger trout and more fishing days.

(Left) A view from the Shinhopple bridge, looking upriver, with Tricos (below) sparkling like stars in the water on an early July morning.

(Overleaf) Below Dutscher's Flats looking downriver on the East Branch, between two deep holes where shad gather and wait before moving upriver in the spring.

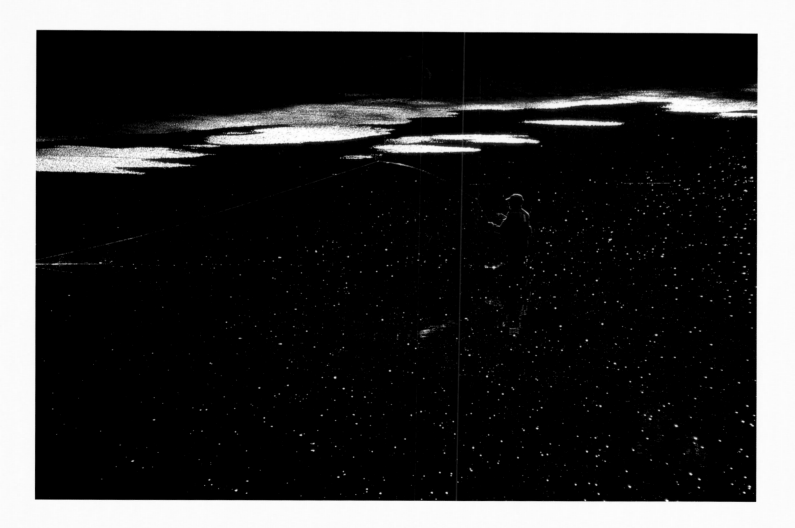

At Upper Airport Pool, an angler fishes to the weedbed in front of the silvery black willow on the far side, where big fish rise in the evenings.

Because of the even temperatures and distribution of food, the fish feed throughout the length of these flat, glassy pools, instead of the heads and tails of pools as they do on the Beaverkill and Willowemoc. The only problem with that is they are very tough to catch. One-quarter of the way down the pool you run out of drift and the fish have too

much time to look at your fly and leader. These conditions defeat most fishermen. The fish are there, but you have to find the flows, and with the riffle sections so short and infrequent, you can drive for a mile past water where you would be unwise to cast a fly.

The lower East Branch—between its junction with the Beaverkill

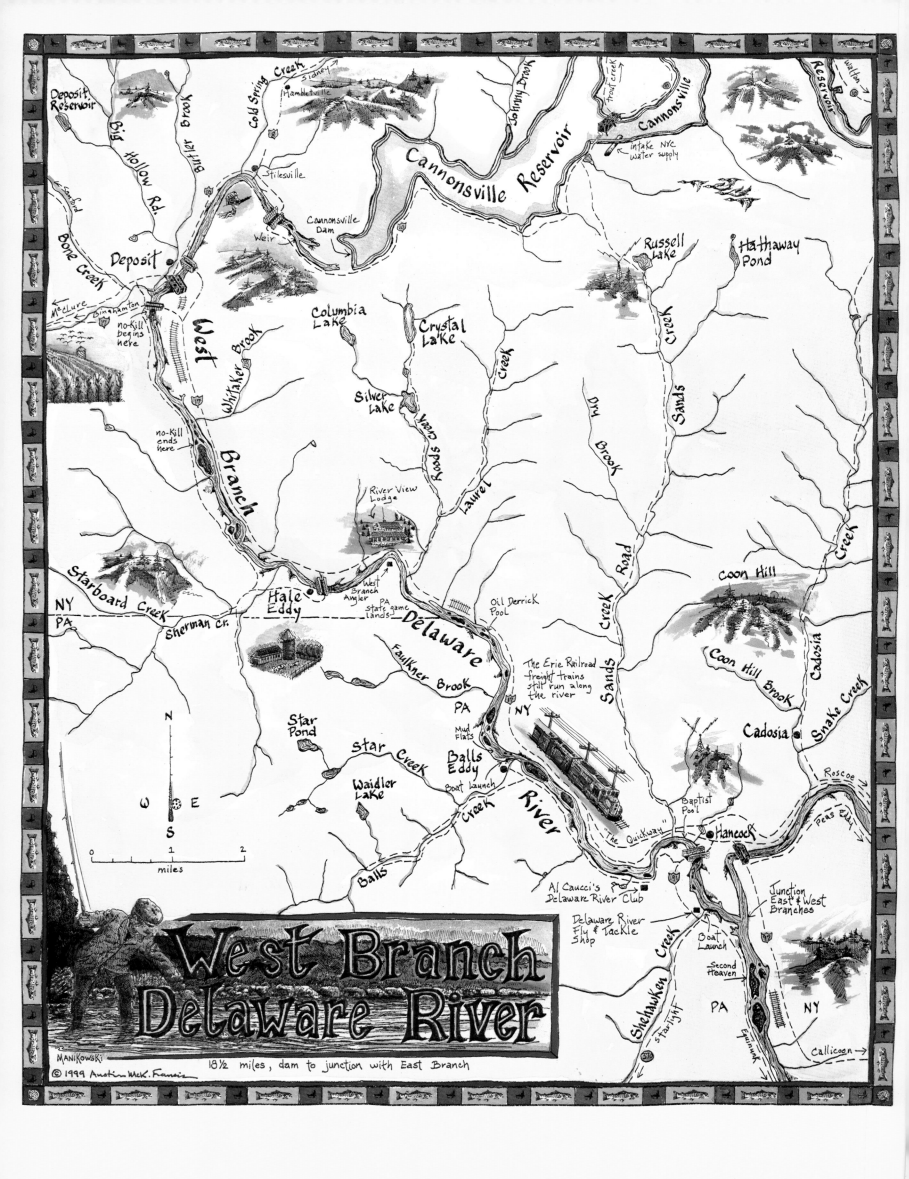

West Branch Delaware River

18½ miles, dam to junction with East Branch

MANIKOWSKI

© 1999 Austin McK. Francis

The no-kill area on the West Branch below Deposit extends from the four-lane highway bridge downriver for two miles; seen here in August when cold-water releases from Cannonsville Reservoir create springlike flows and fishing conditions.
Photograph by Richard Franklin.

and the town of Hancock—resumes the character of a mountain freestone stream. It is once again a river of fluctuating levels and temperatures. Hatches on this 17½-mile section are typical Catskills, plus more green drakes, dobsonflies, and lots of big stoneflies.

Harry Darbee used to fish at daybreak between East Branch village and Fishs Eddy with a cut-down version of the Edson Dark Tiger bucktail to imitate the big stoneflies. One nineteen-incher he caught had eaten several hundred of them. The peak of the hatch when Harry fished it lasted only two or three days and came right after the green drakes.

The dobsonfly and its carnivorous nymph, the hellgrammite, are present in this part of the East Branch and in almost no other Catskill rivers because they like warmer water. On the main Delaware, where they used to thrive, they have dwindled in numbers since the Cannonsville releases began. They can still be found in fair numbers below Callicoon. The dobson is so large that when dusk falls, it is often mistaken for a small bird. It is the eastern equivalent of the salmon fly out west but does not play so important a role for fly fishermen.

There is a story about Bill Kelly and a secret fish he had located on the lower East Branch in the late fifties, before the four-lane highway was completed. Kelly had spotted a really big brown down there and mentioned it to Elsie and Harry Darbee, but didn't say where it was. One night the Darbees were driving along the river and spotted Kelly at

Angler and Deer.
Clustered islets like these below Rood's
Creek break the West Branch into braided
currents, rewarding the angler with
"a target-rich environment."

(Above) Dusk at Shehawken Creek on the West Branch, a half mile before it joins the East Branch to form the main stem of the Delaware River.

(Left) May 24th and the fiddlehead ferns are "popping" on the West Branch below Hale Eddy, a time of year when the fresh bright greens of spring and the classic insect hatches come together—a time for good fishing!

Photograph by Richard Franklin.

the mouth of one of the tributaries, just sitting on the bank and staring into the water, so they knew his fish was right off this trib mouth.

Kelly tied up a six-inch-long muddler and worked hard for several days to catch this fish. One day he had it on but lost it; the next night he came back and another fisherman was there showing off the fish, a beautiful seven-pound brown. He had caught it on a minnow.

In the Hancock Diner, there used to be a big trout on the wall that came out of Peas Eddy. Harry Darbee and Ed Van Put often stopped there when they fished the Delaware. On the windows of the diner would be all the hatch of that day and the night before. It would be simply loaded with flies. Harry used to tell Ed: "Look outside the bars on the window glass and you'll see what's hatching, or when you get to the river in the evening, put your inside car light on with the windows open so the stuff will come in, and you can see that way." Harry rather favored the bar approach.

NINE

Delaware River

〰〰〰〰〰〰〰〰〰〰〰〰

On its main stem, the Delaware is punctuated by long, deep pools called eddies. Some of them are so big and slow of flow that they appear to be mountain lakes. Looking upstream from an eddy, the river bends and a mountain seems to stand directly across the head of the "lake." A view down to the next bend unfolds a like effect; no outlet seems possible.

"Fortunate the angler whose boat nestles softly on the gentle bosom of any of these pools," wrote Robin Ruff in 1889. "His heart will be filled with gladness and his creel with fish, for they are the homes of the small-mouth black bass." Ruff went on to tell of a trip he and a friend took down the Delaware that summer in a flat-bottomed boat. They set out from Hancock supplied with 250 hellgrammites and a mess of lamprey eels for bait.

Drifting and fishing along leisurely, they would anchor at the bottom of a rapid and fish the upper end of an eddy before entering it. In one eddy they caught over one hundred bass, ten of which weighed more than two pounds apiece. Covering five or six miles a day, stopping at small river communities for the night, they fished on down to Lackawaxen, where the Delaware and Hudson Canal Company had a dam that raised the river and formed what raftsmen called the Pond, where they caught "many fine fellows."

Gliding quietly into one of the Delaware's big eddies above Equinunk (left) and the same view (above right) portrayed a hundred years ago in Black Bass Fishing *by artist A. B. Frost.*

The Delaware near Stockport, seen from the New York side (water flowing left) through a mature white pine, now scarce but once the dominant tree along the river in the days before they were nearly all floated down the river as rafts.
Photograph by Richard Franklin.

The fishing trip continued for another five or six miles to Handsome Eddy, "a big one and a dandy for bass." There, almost sixty miles below Hancock, the two fishermen got the canal men—"twenty-five cents will capture the canal chap"—to haul their boat up and place it on the canal boat for the trip back to their starting point.

Now comes the slow and lazy ride back to Lackawaxen, while you lay off to enjoy the fine views and unlimited pipes of the weed. Any man that would ask for a lovelier trip than this from Hancock down would want the earth.

The smallmouth bass Ruff and his friend had been catching were foreigners. In October of 1870, the Erie Railroad, whose tracks ran along the Delaware, transported Ohio River black bass in a perforated basket made to fit the water tank of a locomotive and planted them in the river. The bass took hold and within a few years could be caught throughout the length of the main river and in many of its tributaries as far up as the warmer water prevailed.

The Erie managers considered the Delaware their province and a valuable resource and did everything they could to enhance and promote its attractions. They regularly stocked the many streams that entered the river along their right-of-way, and even hired a New York publicist, Kit Clarke, to write a series of pamphlets for them entitled "Fishing on the Picturesque Erie." In one of them, Clarke wrote about the bass:

Alive and about to swim off, this 17½-inch rainbow is typical of the wild fish in the Delaware; it took a No. 14 Grey Fox.
Photograph by Richard Franklin.

The Delaware is loaded to the muzzle with this fish. No sportsman ever yet held a gun that afforded him an iota of the glorious excitement which thrills a Delaware angler when one of these heavy bass makes a frantic rush and seizes the fly. I have seen men tremble in an ecstasy of agitation until the rod almost fell from their grasp.

Clarke also noted that many trout streams entered the Delaware that did not appear on any maps and described how he had stumbled onto one of them while fishing for bass. Returning the next day, he filled his basket with the "gaudy, crimson-tinted finny fighters." On behalf of the railroad, he urged: "Really good trout brooks, which are so accessible, deserve better patronage. Some day somebody will land on one of these streams and bring out a mess of big trout that will produce a paean of acclaim to make an oratorio seem like a little tin whistle."

An unplanned stocking of the Delaware happened in the 1880s when an Erie train was delayed by a wreck and happened to be carrying several

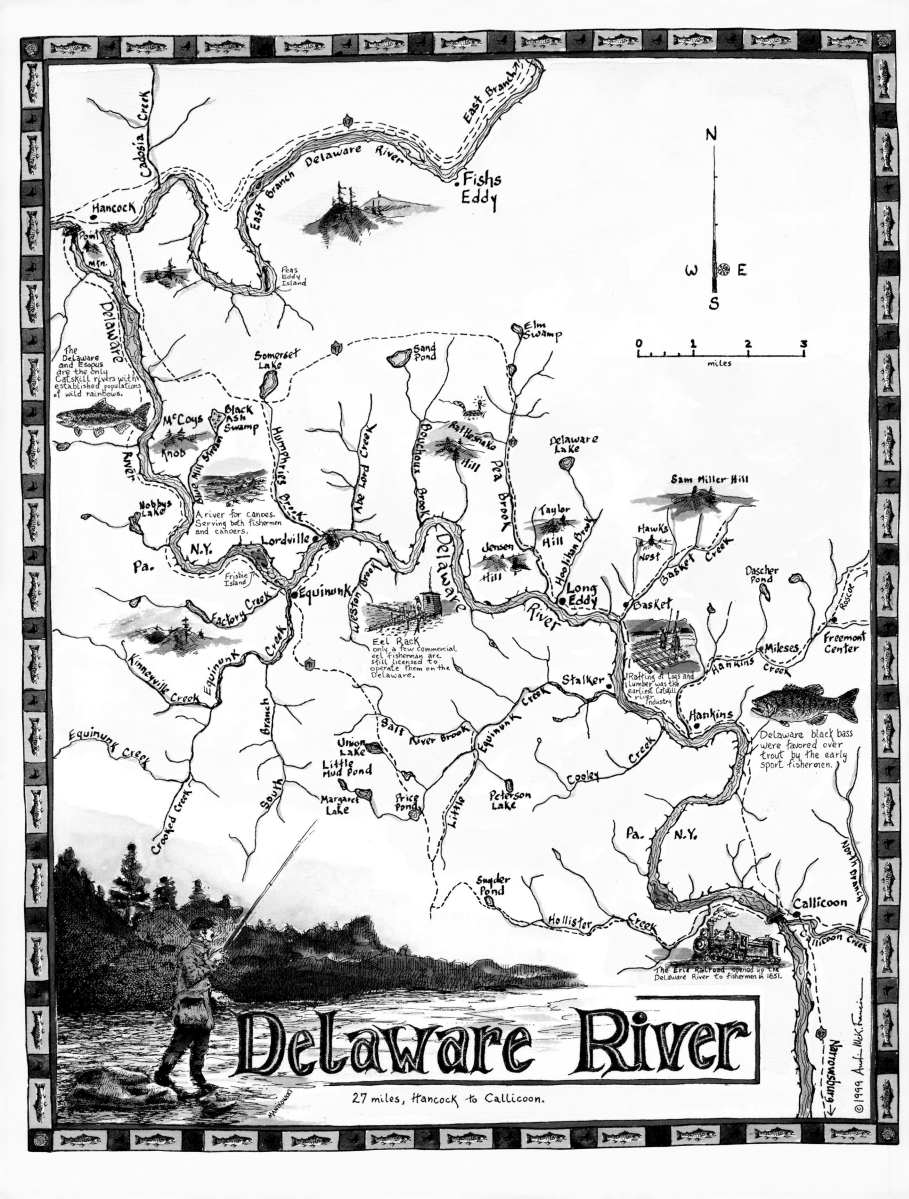

Delaware River

27 miles, Hancock to Callicoon.

Looking upriver at Kellam's Bridge. Sparse Grey Hackle tells the story of a visiting fisherman who was wading steadily downstream beneath the bridge when a man standing on the bridge yelled down, "What're you using, bait or flies?" "A wet fly," shouted the angler. "Okay, then, don't take another step, there's a deep hole just two feet in front of you!"

cans of large rainbow trout. Dan Cahill (no relation to the fly), the brakeman on that run, was worried that the trout would die and persuaded his fellow trainmen to carry the cans a mile or so to Callicoon Creek and dump them in. The trout multiplied, and by 1900 Callicoon Creek was famous for its rainbow fishing.

Rainbows and bass were not the only outsiders to be introduced into the Delaware—just the most successful. Another and rather grand fish-stocking experiment failed completely. For three years beginning in 1871, the Fish Commission of New Jersey planted over 65,000 Atlantic salmon fry in the river. In 1877, 250,000 Pacific salmon fry were put in.

"At last!" said an outdoor reporter in the April 13, 1878, issue of *The Country* as he described the first Atlantic salmon ever caught in the Delaware. It weighed 23½ pounds and was taken near Trenton. "The fish, which is undoubtedly one of the fry placed in the Delaware some six years ago, was in splendid condition. It was forwarded to U.S. Fish Commissioner Baird at the Smithsonian Institution, Washington, where it was viewed by the President and Mrs. Hayes, the Postmaster General and the Secretaries of War and the Navy."

Actually, according to a New Jersey Fish Commission account, seven salmon weighing eight to nine pounds each had been taken out of the

Around the bend from Hankins toward Callicoon. On the far side against those rocks is a nice deep run holding good fish, including walleyes, which are usually caught on lampers or worms.

An early 1930s eel rack, at the apex of a downstream-pointing V-dam that funnels the water—and the eels heading out to sea—into the slatted trap, where they are scooped into holding tanks and sold live or frozen by the rack owner. Only a few licensed eel racks still operate on the Delaware.

Photograph from the N.Y.S. Conservation Department 1935 Annual Report.

Delaware the year before. In 1878, a total of eighteen salmon were killed, the heaviest weighing twenty-four pounds. That same year letters appeared in sporting journals complaining that gill nets set for spring-run shad—many of them illegal—were preventing the salmon from getting upriver in sufficient numbers to establish themselves. None of the correspondents acknowledged that salmon had never existed in rivers as far south as the Delaware. Whatever the cause, after 1878 salmon were never again seen in the Delaware.

With the exception of salmon, the Delaware has welcomed all sorts of fish, among which certainly are its natives, the American eel and the American shad. They share the Delaware in a very interesting manner: eels run out of the Delaware in late fall evenings to spawn in the Sargasso Sea, whereas shad come into the Delaware in early spring, spawning up as far as Harvard and Shinhopple on the East Branch, in some years entering the lower Beaverkill.

Eels are harvested on the Delaware by angling from boats, spearing, and by a few remaining, commercially licensed "eel racks." To spear eels, you wade the shallows at night, usually in September or October. Armed with a strong light and a stout spear, you can spot the eels foraging as they work their way down the river toward the sea. Eel racks are essentially tiers of closely set slats positioned at the point of a huge downstream-pointing

Looking downriver opposite Hankins. In recent years, a few striped bass have been caught in the up-to-twelve-foot-deep run on the opposite bank, using big streamers, zonkers, wooly buggers, usually in low light at dawn and dusk.

A typical Delaware rift: fast water tumbling down a few feet above a bottom strewn with good-sized rocks; excellent holding water, effective with nymphs dredged along the bottom or high-floating attractor flies.

"V" bulldozed into the riverbed to concentrate the flow into and through the rack. The eels are trapped by the slats, scooped out into holding tanks, and sold live or frozen by the rack owner, mostly to European and Japanese eel fanciers.

The shad run varies a lot from year to year, but fisheries biologists have estimated the Delaware's potential shad run at one million fish. The *American Journal of Science and Arts* reported in 1837 that fishermen with shore and drift nets in the lower Delaware caught an estimated 1,500,000 shad annually, and that occasionally more than 10,000 were taken in a single haul.

Shad reach the upper Delaware toward the end of April and continue pressing upstream as the fishermen take their toll. Most of the shad are caught by boat and from the banks on a small lead jig called a shad dart, but fly fishermen have created their own version of the dart, a fluorescent/optic wet-fly pattern that works very well. On light tackle, the shad's acrobatic leaps and runs have earned it the sobriquet of "poor man's salmon." After shad have spawned, they respond more readily to dry flies.

Below Hancock a lot has changed since Robin Ruff's flat-bottomed-boat-and-black-bass days. It is still the same river, but the fashion now is chest waders, dry flies, and wild rainbow trout. The first 27 of the "Big Delaware's" remaining 255 miles to the sea are the ones that interest fly fishermen. This is the river's artificially maintained cold-water zone. It has the same "spring creek" characteristics when releases are in progress as the first 16 miles of the East Branch below the Pepacton Dam; it differs only in that its riffle sections are longer (several hundred feet)

Long cast to a big fish.

and deeper (two to four feet). This is important because the riffles are the aerated, food-producing sections of the river. They also produce the most trout because you can wade to your fish and get a nicely paced, bouncy float over it with your fly.

The regularity of Cannonsville water releases is watched closely by Delaware anglers because water temperature is the single most important factor in determining the quality of fly fishing in the Hancock-to-Callicoon trout zone. Ed Van Put, whose reputation as one of the region's top fly fishermen was built fishing a hundred-plus days each year on the Delaware, vividly explains: "You get a Delaware River fish when the water is 66 degrees, they *explode*—jump and run, down and across, into the backing on one run sometimes. You catch the same fish when it's 72 degrees, and it's a *big* difference. It's hard to believe those few degrees give the fish so much more energy."

Delaware hatches arguably lead the Catskills in variety of species, insect size, and density of a given hatch. There is one fly not even seen on the other rivers and until a few years ago not included in stream entomologies—a big, white mayfly with a little brown spot on the thorax called the August Fly because that's when it hatches. "It hatches here in such numbers," says Van Put, "that when I have been fishing they were plastered along my rod from getting on the line and getting squashed when I stripped them through the guides. The greatest hatches of any fly I have ever seen. You could close your eyes and hold out your hand and you would believe it is snowing!"

The end of another day on the lower Delaware.

The Delaware is the only major Catskill river not stocked with trout; all its trout are wild. From Hancock to Callicoon, browns and rainbows far outnumber the brook trout. The farther downriver you fish, the more rainbows you meet, and the more young ones you find in the tribs; they live there for a year or two and then come down into the big river.

Only two major rivers in the Catskills have established populations of wild rainbows—the Esopus and the Delaware. The rainbow's heritage is that of a sea-run fish; it must have big water to grow up in. On the Esopus, this is the Ashokan Reservoir; on the Delaware, it is the river itself.

Delaware rainbows are tough fish; being wild, they show great individuality and unpredictability. They do not hold position like browns, and they feed at odd times. "You can be in Kellam's Bridge pool tonight, with a good hatch, and maybe a dozen fish are working," says Van Put. "You come tomorrow night and there'll be a hundred, the next night, three hundred! Most fishermen would guess very differently how many fish were in the river based on these different nights.

"When you come over here in an evening you may get ten opportunities to cast to a rising fish. You can't afford to miss them, and you can't afford to lose them when you have them on. You have to be at your best—you have to be in *top shape!*"

PART TWO

Tackle

TEN

Rods

~~~~~~

The modern bamboo fly rod was born in Easton, Pennsylvania, a small town on the Delaware River; passed through its developmental stages in Bangor, Maine; and was perfected and made famous in Central Valley and Highland Mills, New York, neighboring towns in the foothills of the Catskills.

Until about 1840, the best fly rods were made in England. Well-equipped anglers of the day swung ten- to twelve-foot solid rods, exquisitely tapered from lancewood, greenheart, or other resilient woods. It was still the era of "sunk fly" downstream angling, and these twelve-ounce "saplings" were well designed for the task at hand.

Sometime around 1844, **Samuel Phillippe** of Easton began building two- and three-strip fly-rod tip sections out of Calcutta cane to reduce the whippiness and fragility of the long, thin tapers.

Hiram Lewis Leonard
1831–1907

Phillippe had the right combination of talents and interests: he was an accomplished gunsmith and violin maker and an expert trout fisherman. Thaddeus Norris met Phillippe and got the idea for making what became his favorite rod: a white ash butt section, a middle joint of ironwood, and a tip section of four-strip bamboo.

Samuel and his son Solon Phillippe kept experimenting on and improving their rods until, by the late 1850s, they were making a six-strip bamboo rod with twelve-strip handles of alternating hardwood and bamboo. This was the prototype of the American six-strip split-bamboo fly rod that revolutionized the sport of fly fishing.

Hiram L. Leonard built his first fly rod in 1871 in Bangor, Maine. It was of ash and lancewood, and when a Boston sporting-goods house saw it, their agent asked him if he thought he could make the four-strip bamboo rods then so much in demand. Examining the samples the agent had brought with him, Leonard answered, "Yes, and better than those."

He started that same day, in his fortieth year, as a professional rodmaker.

Throughout his early years Leonard had proved himself a man of many skills. He had studied civil engineering and headed the mechanical department for a coal company in Honesdale, Pennsylvania. He had been a master gunsmith; his guns rivaled in beauty and workmanship those of the top gunmakers of the day. And he had learned from his father the craft of oarmaking; the Leonard racing sweeps were prized by rowers even in England. Outdoors, in addition to his fishing, he had been a market hunter of venison and a commercial trapper and fur trader. On top of all that he was an accomplished taxidermist and violinist.

From 1871 on, Hiram Leonard dedicated himself solely and intensively to rodmaking and, over the ensuing thirty-six years until he died, distinguished himself as "the father of the modern split-bamboo fly rod." Having never heard of Samuel Phillippe, Leonard discovered by himself in 1873 the outstanding casting properties of six-strip bamboo construction. In fact, he thought he was the first ever to hit on this idea. What he *can* claim as innovations all took place in his first and most creative ten years as a rodmaker. He invented the first beveling machine to cut rod strips of constant uniformity. This was such an astounding advance and so competitively beneficial that the machine was immediately placed in a locked room and remained off limits except to the most trusted employees for more than seventy-five years.

Leonard was the first to make hexagonally shaped six-strip rods. He discovered by leaving the outside surface of the strips flat, instead of shaving them round, that he retained more of the cane's primary fibers and could thus make a stronger rod. Also during this period, he invented the waterproof and serrated ferrules.

In 1881, three years after he began a partnership with New York tackle dealer William Mills & Son, Leonard moved his operation from Bangor to Central Valley, New York. He brought with him his highly talented employees Hiram and Loman Hawes and recruited Fred E. Thomas, Eustis "Bill" Edwards, and George Varney. In 1885, he persuaded Edward

A corner of the Leonard rodmaking shop in Central Valley. The bearded figure in the right background is H.L. Leonard. Hiram Hawes is second from the left, and E.F. Payne is third from the left.
Courtesy Anglers' Club of New York *Bulletin.*

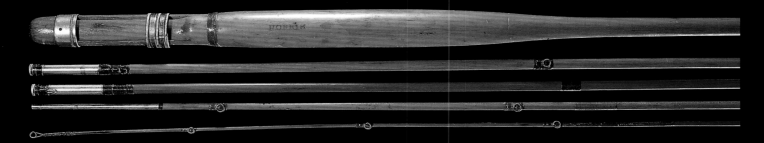

Thad Norris's Rod

12 feet, 5 pieces, 11 ounces; American ash butt, ironwood midsections, "rent and glued" Malacca cane tip.

Norris began making "withy little switches" in the 1850s, which places him among the earliest of American fly-rod builders. In his *American Angler's Book*, he gives detailed instructions to others who "have leisure and a mechanical turn," encouraging them to follow his example in "tackle-making . . . as a pleasant recreation."
Courtesy Anglers' Club of New York.

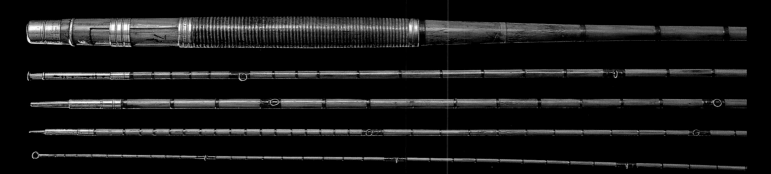

Charles F. Murphy

1865; 12 feet, 3 pieces (two tips and two midsections), 8 ounces; American ash butt; split, glued, and rounded Calcutta cane mid- and tip sections.

Murphy, based in Newark, New Jersey, was this country's first commercial rodbuilder and is credited by rod historian Martin Keane with weaning American anglers from their dependency on English bamboo rods.
Courtesy American Museum of Fly Fishing.

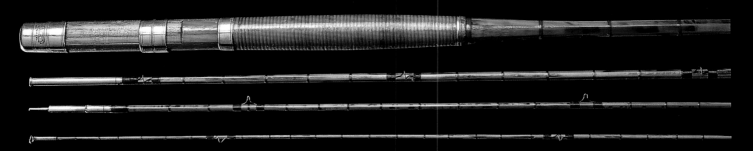

H.L. Leonard

1873; 11 feet, 3 pieces (two tips), 8 ounces. Rattan grip, Calcutta bamboo with its characteristic brown dappling, caused by exporters who flame-straightened the typically crooked Calcutta for ease of shipping. Snake line guides have replaced the original folding ring guides that were phased out on better rods after 1895.
Courtesy American Museum of Fly Fishing.

H.L. Leonard

c.1875; 7-piece pack rod with 21½-inch fitted case; can be assembled as an 8½-foot, 5-piece, 5-ounce rod, or as a 10-foot-3-inch, 6-piece, 5½-ounce rod (with two tips). The stamp of John Krider, a Philadelphia gun and fishing tackle dealer, appears on the butt cap.

Short rods, wrote Thad Norris, "can be conveniently carried in a travelling trunk if made in pieces of two feet . . . but should have short ferrules so the elasticity of the rod is less impaired."
Courtesy Anglers' Club of New York.

F. Payne to come down and join the group. No more high-powered aggregation of rodbuilding talent has ever since been assembled under one roof. These men were so skilled individually that each except Varney eventually started a rod business of his own.

The H.L. Leonard Rod Company in its new location was just fifty miles north of Mills's store and only twenty-five miles east of the famed Catskill rivers that were to be the proving grounds for Leonard's emerging series of new rod designs. According to rod historian Martin Keane, in his book *Classic Rods and Rodmakers*, the "first and foremost of the early super-Leonards was his Catskill series, which featured the lightest and daintiest rods available." The "Catskill" came out in 1883 at 9½ feet and 4⅝ ounces, followed by the "Petite Catskill" in 1890 at 9½ feet and 3⅛ ounces, only to be topped in 1894 by the wispy "Fairy Catskill" at 8 feet, 2 inches, and an incredibly light 2 ounces. A number of these were shipped to England, and the Catskill series in general was a major force in popularizing lightweight fly rods.

By the turn of the century, in response to the growing use of dry flies, Leonard designed a series of new rod tapers and came out with a battery of fast-recovery dry-fly rods, which caught on quickly among his clientele. On the wings of William Mills's publicity and salesmanship, the Leonard name soared to fame among anglers. He bragged justifiably: "My rods took the first prize at Vienna, London, and at the world's fair, Philadelphia, and in all contests for fly, or bait casting, they lead the world."

Perhaps the highest praise he received was bestowed on Leonard by G.E.M. Skues, the noted English author and wet-fly authority. He became a faithful Leonard customer and was so fond of one particular nine-footer that he often referred to it in his angling books as "W.B.R."— World's Best Rod.

For unknown reasons, most of Leonard's skilled employees left him in 1889 and 1890 to make rods on their own. Measured by years in business and rods produced, **Edward F. Payne** was by far the most successful of these men. After working with various combinations of partners and owners, Payne bought controlling interest in his business and moved it in 1898 to Highland Mills, New York, just two miles up the road from his old employer in Central Valley.

Ed Payne won acclaim for his precision craftsmanship and close attention to the finest details in a custom rod. His all-silver, full-metal reel seats were so highly polished and elegantly formed that they ranked in a class with fine jewelry. The rods themselves were immaculately varnished, accented in silk by his hallmark jasper-and-red-tipped windings, with the glue lines so well concealed that the cane strips appeared to have grown together conveniently in their hexagonal, tapered sections.

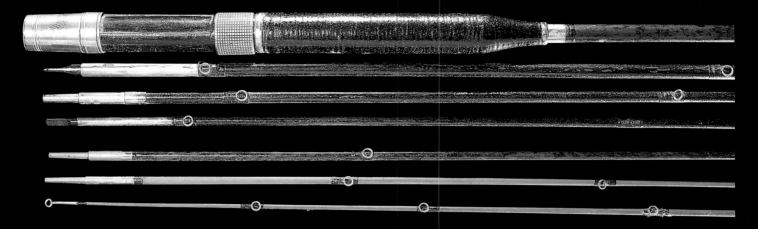

William Mitchell

c.1885; 8 pieces. Greenheart, multi-purpose rod with detachable handle—an 1883 Mitchell patent—allowing different midsections and tips to be joined to suit varying fishing situations.

Tips are of Malacca cane, and reel band has Mitchell's singular checkered patterning.
Courtesy Anglers' Club of New York.

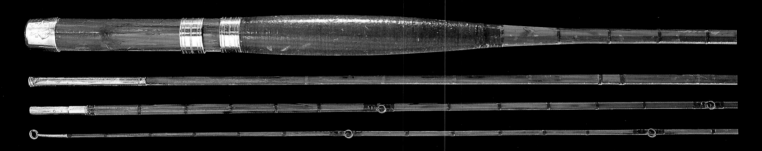

Thomas H. Chubb

c.1890; 8 feet, 1 inch, 2 pieces (with two tips), 3¾ ounces.
Six-strip bamboo, flat-faced rattan grip with interwoven red thread. Chubb patented a full-drawn metal reel seat in 1880, with raised guide rails on the seat to keep the reel from twisting. He was one of the major builders of fine rods in the late 1800s; his metal-stamped trademark star—normally a decal on the wood—is rare.
Courtesy Anglers' Club of New York.

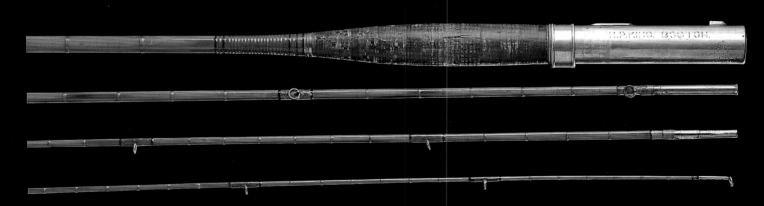

H. L. Leonard

1885; 9 feet, 3 pieces, 5 ounces.

One of the first of the Catskill series, which were influential in bringing about the switch to lighter fly rods.
Courtesy American Museum of Fly Fishing.

Ed Payne made a special rod for Theodore Gordon around 1895—a 9½ footer, three pieces, with a wet-fly action. Gordon tied thirty-nine dozen trout flies to pay for it. In 1912, he gave it to Herman Christian, saying, "I don't know of anybody who would appreciate it as much as you would." Christian fished with it until the late 1940s and then sold it back to the E.F. Payne Rod Co. for its museum. Wendle ("Tom") Collins bought E.F. Payne shortly after that and eventually presented the rod to the Anglers' Club of New York, where it was destroyed, along with several other historic rods in a display case, by a terrorist's bomb in 1975.

Jim Payne began as an apprentice in his father's Highland Mills shop when he was ten years old. In 1914, when he was twenty-one, his father died and Jim took over the family rodmaking business. Like his father, Jim Payne was a perfectionist, always looking for ways to improve his rods. Soon after he was on his own, young Payne invented a special tool, sort of a hot-iron clamp, with which he squeezed the leaf nodes down into line with the rest of the cane strip, thereby avoiding the filing away and weakening of the strip. Other rodmakers copied the idea for a while, but then gave it up as too time consuming.

Over the next ten years, Payne developed a two-step process of flame tempering and oven curing the bamboo strips that made his rods considerably more resilient and powerful. The heat treatments also turned his rods a rich, deep brown, a characteristic that came to distinguish Payne rods from those of his competitors.

Other innovations by Jim Payne included, in 1925, a locking reel seat designed mainly by new employee and master metalsmith George Halstead; a new generation of "parabolic action" fly rods in the 1930s, based on the suggestions of French angler and rod designer Charles Ritz;

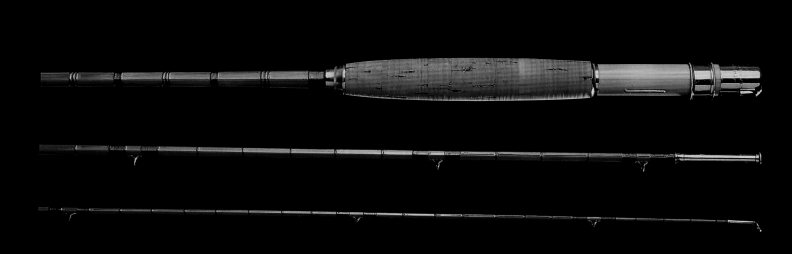

Kosmic Rod Co.

1890; 8½ feet, 3 pieces (with two tips), 3½ ounces.
An early Kosmic, creation of Hiram Leonard's protégés, Fred Thomas, Bill Edwards, and Loman Hawes. Its innovations included an ivory-like cellulose reel seat and a revolutionary ferrule with a celluloid collar in the throat to absorb flexing pressures. This example has the newly popular snake guides instead of folding rings, and rails on the reel seat to keep the reel aligned.
Courtesy Catskill Fly Fishing Center.

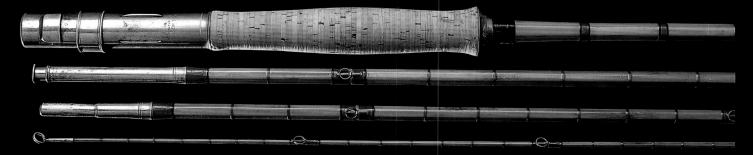

Kosmic Rod Co.

1894; 10 feet, 4 pieces, 10 ounces; hexagonal, six-strip Tonkin bamboo.

This hefty Kosmic, with its special flex-dampening collar, was a favorite in the casting tournaments of the day.

Courtesy American Museum of Fly Fishing.

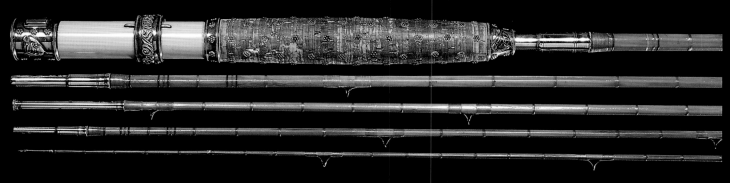

Kosmic Rod Co.

1895; 9 feet, 5 inches, 3 joints plus handle (two midsections and three tips), 7 ounces. A sterling silver presentation rod, with silver work by Durand & Co., including florets embedded in the cork grip.

Jim Brown, observing the sharp-toothed trout heads on the reel band and seat, said, "They were not just making a rod to go fishing, they were making a statement about their craft."

Courtesy Anglers' Club of New York.

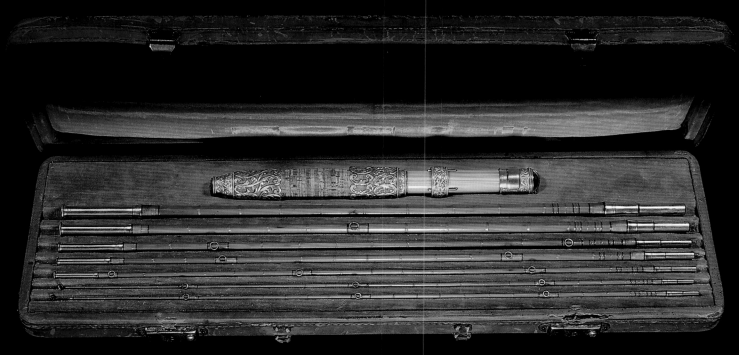

Kosmic Rod Co.

1895; 9 feet, 7 inches, 6 joints plus handle (with two tips), 9 ounces. New York philanthropist Charles M. Pratt heard that Queen Victoria had once received a gold fly rod and got a case of rod envy, so he ordered his own out of flawless Calcutta cane, decorated by goldsmiths Durand & Co. The only gold Kosmic known to exist, it was not designed to be, and never has been, fished.

Courtesy Anglers' Club of New York.

a series of special-purpose rods for canoe casting and another series for streamer fishing. He even built a four-foot, four-inch "Banty Payne," presumably to suit a woman angler with designs on large steelhead.

Jim Payne was a well-known figure on Catskill streams. His fishing friends included Ed Hewitt, Roy Steenrod, and two up-and-coming rod-makers, Pinky Gillum and Everett Garrison. He also fished with and made rods for A.E. Hendrickson. In fact, Hendrickson was Jim Payne's biggest customer, especially during the Depression. There was most likely a feeling of compassion for a fellow angler whose orders were running thin, but Hendrickson was a perfectionist himself, and he once had Jim Payne build forty-seven ten-foot salmon rods before he was finally satisfied with no. 48.

Jim Payne outside his rod shop.
Photograph by Cleve Speer, courtesy Clear Lake Club.

Jim Payne walked out of his shop in May of 1968 saying that he didn't know when he would be back. He died a month later after sixty-four years of rodmaking. His and his father's joint careers in the E.F. Payne Rod Company spanned ninety-two years and resulted in some of the finest split-cane rods ever made.

H.S. "Pinky" Gillum learned how to make rods pretty much on his own. After a brief indoctrination by expert rodmaker Bill Edwards—one of Hiram Leonard's original "Central Valley Six"—Gillum progressed steadily in his own self-reliant manner to become an extraordinarily talented rodbuilder. The way he became an instant flytier was typical of Gillum's independence and determination: two weeks after a single half-hour lesson from Harry Darbee, Gillum returned with flies of such exceptional quality that Harry tried to persuade him to be a flytying professional also.

From his rod shop in Ridgefield, Connecticut, Pinky Gillum turned out some two thousand rods from 1923 to 1966. He was working on three

*Vern Heyney holding one of the first rods designed and made by Everett
Garrison, who sent it up to Heyney on the Beaverkill for testing in 1933.
The rod was so successful that everyone Heyney showed it to wanted one
also, resulting in forty orders for Garrison before the summer was over.*
Courtesy Hoagy B. Carmichael.

rods the day he died; his wife, Winnie, finished and delivered them. He was not primarily an innovator, but he probably had no peer for consistent output of top-quality bamboo rods. With his wife as his only helper, he did everything himself except make his own ferrules. When he strung up a finished rod, he tried it on the lawn; if he didn't like it, he was known occasionally to take the rod apart, hold the sections together, and break them over his knee. Such persistence extended even to his feelings about how customers used his rods. "They are buying two weeks of my life," he would say, and if he could tell that a rod had been damaged through wanton neglect, Pinky simply refused to repair it. On one occasion he yanked a brand-new Gillum away from a startled angler who was jerking it to free a hung-up fly, gave him back his money, and stalked off the stream.

Pinky Gillum could be understood best as a professional's professional. He was truly at ease with only the most knowledgeable anglers who knew and could appreciate what he was trying to achieve. He would not give interviews to outdoor writers and did not believe in advertising. He felt that a good product would advertise itself, and this was certainly true in the case of Gillum fly rods. After the first few years of rodbuilding, he always had more orders than he could fill. Harry Darbee's fly shop in Roscoe was Gillum's only "official" retail outlet.

The list of famous anglers who were loyal Gillum customers is long. Jack Atherton—angler, author, and artist—said, "If I could have only one rod, I would ask Pinky Gillum to make it for me." Harry Darbee fished with one Gillum rod that he would never consider selling. "This rod I'm taking in my coffin," he said. "They say there's fishing in the Styx."

Gillum was a loner and very secretive about his rodbuilding methods; he had no protégé. When he died, his widow sold his "book of tapers," equipment, and Tonkin cane to rodmaker Minert Hull.

For **Everett Garrison,** rodmaking began as a hobby and became an all-consuming avocation. He had grown up in Yonkers, New York, and fished the Esopus as a boy. Throughout the 1920s, he made bamboo rods for his own use. Then he had the good fortune to meet his neighbor, Dr. George Parker Holden, who made and collected rods and had written a definitive book on them, *The Idyl of the Split-Bamboo.* Holden's encouragement and knowledge from having studied the great master Hiram Leonard's techniques were invaluable to Garrison in his early rodmaking efforts.

The turning point came with the Depression, when Garrison and his fishing friend Vernon Heyney both lost their jobs at the New York Central Railroad. Heyney went to the Beaverkill to live and fish; Garrison went down to his basement to make rods. His degree and professional background as a structural engineer then came into full play as he took on the ambitious task of scientifically redesigning the split-bamboo rod.

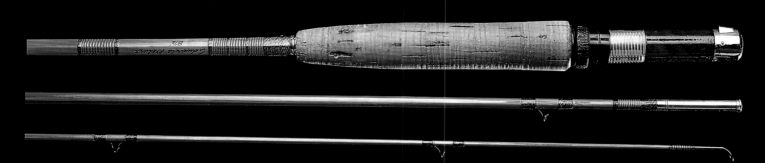

Eustis W. (Bill) Edwards

c.1926; 8½ feet "Deluxe," 3 pieces, 4½ ounces.
Bill Edwards developed the technique of heat treating Tonkin cane strips before they were beveled and joined into rods, "transforming them into steely springs of unprecedented strength and resiliency," wrote Martin Keane. Thus Edwards's rods were lighter yet stronger than their predecessors.
Courtesy Catskill Fly Fishing Center

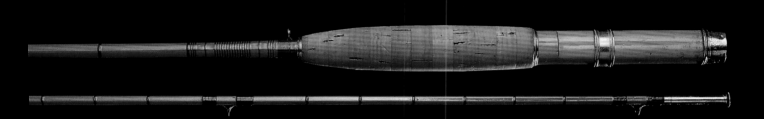

H.L. Leonard

c.1905; 8 feet, 3 pieces, 2⅞ ounces; made for George M.L. LaBranche.
A very light rod for its vintage; snake guides, tiny signature wraps, standard sliding-band, butternut reel seat.
Courtesy Catskill Fly Fishing Center.

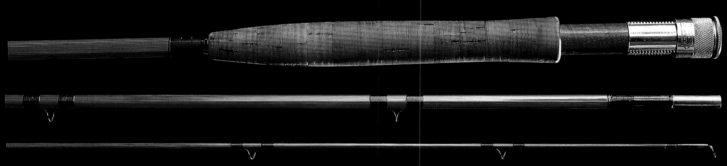

Harold S. (Pinky) Gillum

c.1948; 9 feet, 3 pieces (with two tips), 6 ounces; made for Art Flick.
Gillum is supposed to have learned rodbuilding from Bill Edwards by observing and retaining most of what he saw (he learned flytying from Harry Darbee this way). Gillum built rods of great power through two innovations: oven tempering bamboo and the use of synthetic glue, which gave his rods a distinctive straw-colored finish and dark-rose glue lines.
Courtesy Catskill Fly Fishing Center.

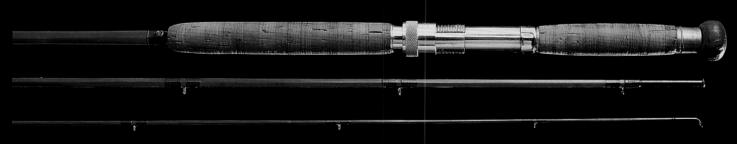

Jim Payne

c.1930; 10-foot salmon rod, 3 pieces (with two tips and butt extension), 8½ ounces.
The E.F. Payne Rod Company, begun by Jim's father, Ed, made fine bamboo rods for ninety-two years. Jim began with flame tempering and switched to a kiln to strengthen the cane strips, producing rods with a characteristic rich deep-brown finish. Other advances: he invented a tool that pressed leaf nodes into line with the rest of the strip, and designed with George Halstead a highly polished aluminum locking reel seat.
Courtesy Catskill Fly Fishing Center.

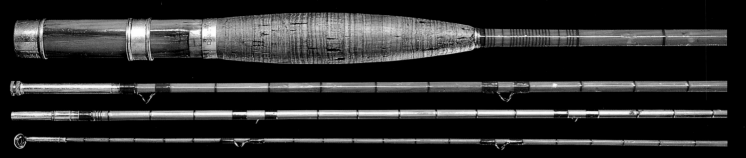

H.L. Leonard

c.1930; 8 feet, 5 inches, 3 pieces (with two tips), 4 ounces; made for Mildred von Kienbusch. Ownership band built into bottom of the *diminutive grip, agate tiptop and small snake guides for delicate line, tiny signature winds in front of grip; all very feminine.*

Courtesy Anglers' Club of New York.

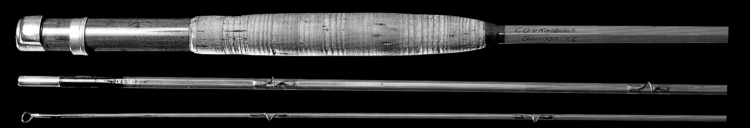

Everett Garrison

1936; 8 feet, 2 pieces (with two tips), 4.4 ounces; made for Carl Otto von Kienbusch.

Though he considered himself an amateur, Garrison crafted some 700 of the finest rods in forty years of spare time. When Garrison was just getting started, Kienbusch invited him to bring his rods to the Anglers' Club and tell how he built them. Club members bought nineteen of the twenty he had, "save for one seven-footer that I used for the rest of my fishing life."

Courtesy American Museum of Fly Fishing.

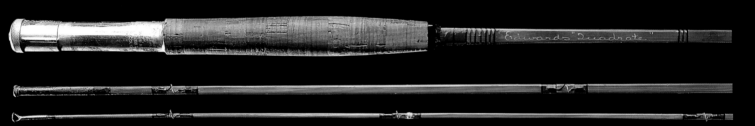

W.E. Edwards Quadrate

1938; 9 feet, 3 pieces, 6 ounces.

The four-strip Quad was created by Eustis's son; it was designed for power (Quads require heavier lines than six-strip rods of comparable length and weight) and, supporters claimed, gave more control and accuracy. The reel seat on this rod, originally molded black plastic, has been replaced by an uplocking metal seat.

Courtesy American Museum of Fly Fishing.

H.L. Leonard "Baby Catskill"

c.1940; 6 feet, 2 pieces (with two tips), 1 ounce.

This wisp of a rod was made partly to show off the rodbuilder's skill and is, as far as is known, the world's lightest fishable six-strip rod; the grip is barely large enough for an adult hand, and it tapers at the tiptop to hairlike thinness.

Courtesy Wayne W. McFarland, Jr.

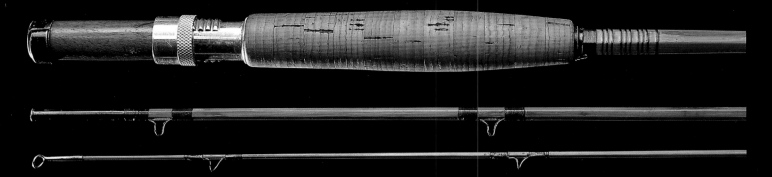

F. E. Thomas Rod Company

1947; 8½ feet, 3 pieces, 5 ounces.

For sixty years (1898–1958), the Thomas rod company—first under Fred, then his son Leon—made fine split-cane rods distinguished by rich dark finishes, blue-black gunmetal fittings, and signature groupings of thin-band silk windings. The company was known less for innovation than for its consistent high-quality craftsmanship.

Courtesy American Museum of Fly Fishing.

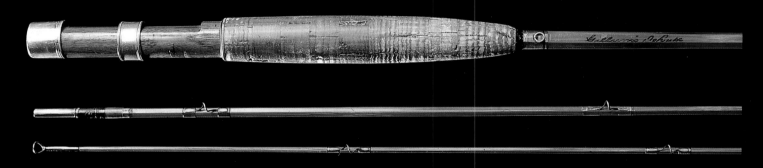

Harold S. (Pinky) Gillum

1948; 7 feet, 2 pieces (with two tips), 3 ounces.

Custom-made for Maxine Atherton, especially for trout, with transparent wraps and sliding-band reel seat, neither of which was customary on Gillum rods.

Courtesy American Museum of Fly Fishing.

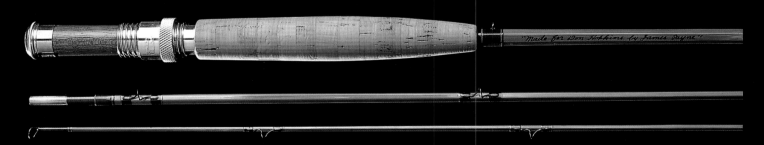

Jim Payne

1965; 7½ feet, 2 pieces (with two tips), 4½ ounces; made for Don Hopkins.

An unusual Payne in that it is inscribed to the owner, including a special decorative butt cap. Jim Payne died three years after he made this rod, ending ninety-two years of excellence at the E.F. Payne Rod Company.

Courtesy American Museum of Fly Fishing.

Rodmakers before Garrison had worked out their rod actions and tapers by trial and error, but Garrison undertook nothing less than a full-scale analysis of the physical properties of bamboo, its capabilities and limitations under stress, and the resulting rod tapers for different kinds of fishing that could produce in each case the most efficient delivery of the fly.

Besides the tapers, which Garrison calculated in thousandths of an inch, there had to be a delicate balance between the cane and its moisture content, the glue, ferrules, guides, windings, and finish. Garrison called the rod action that resulted from all these components working in harmony a "progressive action." What this means is that at the moment the power stroke begins, the energy passing from the wrist into the lowest flexing point in the rod should travel at an absolutely even speed but with steadily diminishing force up the rod into the unfolding line until the leader has straightened out, the fly is hovering over its target, and the force has diminished to zero.

By midsummer of 1932, Garrison had fashioned two eight-foot rods based on his new theories. One he gave to John Alden Knight, of Solunar Table renown; the other he sent to Vernon Heyney on the Beaverkill. Heyney had difficulty getting used to the new action, so accustomed was he to the conventional tapers of his favorite Payne rods, but he persisted and, with adjustments in his casting, he eventually laid aside his Paynes and became a permanent Garrison convert. By the end of the summer, Heyney had proselytized enough friends and acquaintances on the stream to send Garrison more than forty orders for identical rods.

Dan Brenan, from Syracuse, a fine rodmaker in his own right, was one of Heyney's converts. Brenan thought the new Garrison was "a sweetheart: trim, neat, superbly finished, and with a masculinity of action that belies the svelte femininity of appearance."

The Garrison rod was indeed more powerful than it looked. Its moderately tapered grip, light straw color, transparent windings, and visible glue lines between strips all conveyed an image of functional austerity. Nothing went into the rod that did not enhance its performance. It was what you would expect from an engineering genius bent on creating the ultimate casting instrument.

Unlike Gillum, Garrison did pass his knowledge and craft on to a protégé. **Hoagy B. Carmichael,** soon after meeting Garrison, was drawn to the excellence and dedication of the master rodbuilder. Working for several years alongside Garrison, Carmichael: learned his highly technical approach; began coauthoring the book *A Master's Guide to Building a Bamboo Fly Rod;* and after Garrison's death, completed the book and went on to build fine bamboo rods in the Garrison tradition.

Walt Carpenter is one of the last full-time handcrafted-bamboo rodbuilders in the Leonard tradition. He worked for the Leonard Rod Company in the 1970s, as well as for Jim Payne, whom Carpenter considers "the most accomplished rodmaker" he's ever known. Carpenter got involved in rodbuilding, he says, "because I wanted to be a perpetuator more than a maker. I was more interested in the history of the rod companies and their craftsmen than in making rods, but to really achieve that goal I had to become a rodbuilder myself."

In the late 1960s, Carpenter rescued from a rust pile the 1890 bamboo-strip beveler built by Loman Hawes in launching his partnership with Fred Thomas and Eustis Edwards, all three of whom had worked for and learned their trade from Hiram Leonard. Thomas, Edwards, and Hawes were the creators of the legendary Kosmic rods.

In reflecting on his heritage, Carpenter says, "I've borrowed from Leonard, Edwards, Thomas, but mainly Jim Payne, in building the Carpenter rod. It's this continuity, I think, that holds all of the Catskill rodmakers together—though we're spread out all over the place—in a wonderfully close-knit community."

ELEVEN
Reels

~~~~~~~~~~~~~~~~~~~

When American sport fishing was in its early stages in the mid-1800s, most fishing tackle—including reels—was being imported from England. By the time American reel designers and makers started "doing their own thing," two centers of reelmaking had emerged—New York and Kentucky. The New York and Kentucky reels were quite unlike each other.

The New York reels usually had a handle with a ball-shaped counterweight opposite the knob and came to be known as "ball-handle" reels. They were first made for saltwater fishing and then were scaled down for lake and stream fishing. The New York reelmakers were typically machinists, and their products were models of industrial simplicity, no frills.

By contrast, Kentucky reelmakers were jewelers and watchmakers. Their reels had a sophisticated, artistic look with fine detailing, and were made for the freshwater fisherman. Larger sizes were for bass; smaller sizes, down to 1⅝ inches, were for trout and fly fishing.

New York and Kentucky reelmakers had both improved on the old-fashioned British multiplying reels they had used as models, but were still lagging in design and production of the light, single-action reels that were to become the reels of choice among growing ranks of fly fishermen. Enter the Billinghurst reel.

William Billinghurst, expert gunsmith, lived in Rochester, New York, just fifteen miles north of Caledonia, where Seth Green was pioneering in the science of fish culture. Following the Civil War, Billinghurst, beating swords into plowshares, converted a share of his production to fishing reels. Having patented his new reel design in 1859, Billinghurst began turning them out in quantity after the war. It was America's first single-action fly reel, an open-frame design of brass spokes and perimeter that invited its popular name, "birdcage reel." It had a narrow spool and wide core that recovered line faster than other single-action reels. Its open

William Mills & Son

c.1881; patent prototype for the 1882 planetary gear fly reel, brass, triple multiplier, 4 x 1½ inches, 16½ ounces.

Planetary gears eliminated the offset handle of most multipliers and the chance of fly-line fouling. Rather heavy for fishing and mechanically complex, the reel was never a commercial success.

Courtesy Catskill Fly Fishing Center.

G.C. Furman

1826; salmon or saltwater reel, 3 x 1 ½ inches, 16 ounces.

Brass, double multiplier. Furman owned the reel; the maker, though unknown, is believed to have been in New York City; the oldest reel of known age in the AMFF collection, rebuilt in 1838.

Courtesy American Museum of Fly Fishing.

F. Vom Hofe & Son

c.1865; brass, ball-handle multiplier, size 5, used for light bait or fly fishing, 1⅞ x 1¼ inches, 6 ounces.

Frederick Vom Hofe, father of Edward and Julius, began the family business of making fishing reels in 1857 in Manhattan.

Courtesy Anglers' Club of New York.

T.H. Bate & Co.

c.1870; brass, crank handle, single-action bait or fly reel, 2 x 1 inches, 3¾ ounces.

T.H. Bate & Co., one of the earliest New York tackle dealers, published a fishing-tackle catalog in 1867, before it became William Mills & Son in 1875.

Courtesy Anglers' Club of New York.

Andrew Clerk & Co.

c.1865; ball-handle reel, brass double multiplier, light saltwater or salmon reel, 2½ x 1⅞ inches, 13⅜ ounces.

Clerk, which became Abbey and Imbrie in 1875, may also have made this reel. The New York ball-handle style emerged in the 1830s and remained popular into the 1880s.

Courtesy American Museum of Fly Fishing.

Thaddeus Norris

1864; brass single-action, fixed-click, 2 x ⅞ inches, 4 ounces.

Norris, author of *The American Angler's Book*, made this reel for Wallace (Chancellor) Gould Levison, a member of the Brooklyn Fly Fishers and founding member of the Anglers' Club of New York. The only known Norris reel.

Courtesy Anglers' Club of New York.

William Mills & Son

1885; trout-size model of the 1882 patent planetary gear reel, bronze and nickel-silver, triple multiplier, 2¼ x ¾ inches, 4 ounces.

Raised-pillar fly reel with automatic drag that engaged only as line was pulled from the reel.

Courtesy Anglers' Club of New York.

William Mills & Son

c.1885; brass click reel with protective front rim, 2½ x ⅞ inches, 4⅜ ounces.

Referred to in its day as the "Mills patent winch."

Courtesy Catskill Fly Fishing Center.

Julius Vom Hofe

c.1920 (October 8, 1889, patent); size 3, single-action fly reel, nickel-silver and dark brown hard-rubber sideplates, counterbalanced handle, fixed click, raised pillars, 2 x 1 inches, 4 ounces. Retailer's name stamped on front: "Von Lengerke & Detmold, New York."

Courtesy Anglers' Club of New York.

frame allowed for faster drying of the silk lines then in use. Also, in a radical departure for fishing reels, it attached *sideways* to the rod. The Billinghurst reel inspired a series of sidemount siblings, from other makers, that held the favor of anglers into the late 1800s before they gradually lost out to the more standard vertical-mount reels.

The Charles F. Orvis 1874 Patent Reel was another unique design; it was flat as a pancake, with multiple perforations in its chrome-plated sideplates. Its very narrow spool took up line faster than most of the reels then on the market. The Orvis reel was an immediate hit. It sold steadily for some forty years and is considered the first modern American fly reel.

Hiram Leonard, already well known for his split-bamboo rods, entered the reel business in 1877 with his raised-pillar, bronze-and-nickel-silver ("bi-metal") reel, patented by Francis Philbrook, who assigned the patent to Leonard. The earliest Leonard bi-metals were made by Philbrook and Edward F. Payne in Maine. By 1900, the manufacturing was transferred to the shop of Julius Vom Hofe in New York City, where it remained until World War II. The Leonard reel's sound construction and classy good looks made it a favorite among anglers for over sixty years.

The first successful automatic fly reel was patented in 1880 by Francis A. Loomis, who lived in Onondaga, a small town just outside Syracuse, New York. Reuben Wood, a famous tournament caster and originator of the Reub Wood fly, used it and gave it a testimonial. Around 1885, Loomis's company was sold to Yawman & Erbe, Rochester, New York, which continued to make the Loomis reel. Y&E was then sold in 1915 to Horrocks-Ibbotson, which eventually folded under strong competition from the Martin Reel Company (formerly the Martin Automatic Fishing Reel Co.) of Mohawk, New York. The Martin Reel Co. is America's oldest surviving reel company, having made automatic reels continuously since 1892.

Because of its extra weight, high-maintenance complexity, and the perception held by some that it endows the angler with an unsporting mechanical advantage, the automatic reel has drawn criticism; however, it still goes on, over one hundred years in service, particularly among solo, boat-borne fishers who must manage their craft and cast at the same time, and among handicapped anglers.

Edward Vom Hofe, a contemporary of Hiram Leonard, whose father, Frederick, had begun making the New York ball-handle multipliers in Manhattan in the 1850s, was one of America's best-known and most respected reelmakers. The Vom Hofe family moved to Brooklyn in 1866, and the following year son Edward at the age of twenty-one started his own company and trademark in high-quality reels. Edward's older

Evolution of the Edward Vom Hofe "Peerless" Trout Reel

Vom Hofe was a perfectionist, as were many nineteenth-century handcraftsmen involved in designing and making fishing tackle. He strove continually to improve his product. This series of reels, with approximate dates, gives a rare look at the Peerless model's progressive development. All four measure 2⅛ x ¾ inches, with varying weights.

From the collection of Hoagy B. Carmichael.

c.1870;
4.8 ounces; all
nickel-silver, crank
handle, fixed click, heavy for its size,
line sometimes caught under handle.

c.1875;
3.1 ounces;
hard-rubber side-
plates, improved crank han-
dle, fixed click, much lighter but subject
to breaking.

c.1880;
3.2 ounces;
recessed crank handle
alleviated the line-tangling; nickle-
silver rims protected the hard-rubber
sideplates; fixed click.

c.1890;
3.25 ounces;
recessed and
counterbalanced,
S-shaped handle; nickel-
silver protective rims; and adjustable click.

A.H. Fowler Gem

c.1872 (June 18, 1872, patent); black hard rubber with brass fittings, 3 x ¾ inches, 1.2 ounces.

One of the early sidemounts, designed by an Ithaca, New York, dentist.

Courtesy Catskill Fly Fishing Center.

A.H. Fowler "Improved Gem"

c.1875; 1.3 ounces, nickel-plated fittings; this model has a fixed click.

The Gems were probably the lightest usable fly reels ever made, but they were very fragile and few have survived.

Courtesy Hoagy B. Carmichael.

Charles M. Clinton

c.1900 (October 29, 1889, patent); nickel-silver sidemount, internal fixed click, 2⅝ x ¾ inches, 3 ounces.

Clinton, an Ithaca, New York, inventor, clearly modeled his reel on the Fowler Gem but used all metal to solve the fragility problem.

Courtesy Catskill Fly Fishing Center.

Edward P. Follett

c.1885; nickel-plated brass sidemount, no click or drag, 3½ x ½ inches, 3 ounces.

A Rochester tinsmith and lantern maker, Follett was one of the upstate New York sidemount reelmakers.

Courtesy American Museum of Fly Fishing.

William Billinghurst

c.1865 (August 9, 1859, patent); brass wire and castings, 3 x ¾ inches, 3¼ ounces.

Billinghurst was a Rochester gunsmith. His "birdcage" reel, ventilated thus to speed the drying of silk fly lines, is considered to be the first American fly reel.

Courtesy Catskill Fly Fishing Center.

H.L. Leonard

c.1880 (June 12, 1877, patent); bronze and nickel-silver "bi-metal" raised-pillar reel, 2⅝ x 1 inches, 5 ounces.

Made until 1917; this example was owned by Charles B. Boynton, a founding member of the Brooklyn Fly Fishers.

Courtesy Catskill Fly Fishing Center.

H.L. Leonard

c.1878; nickel-silver raised-pillar, single-action, crank handle, fixed-click trout reel, marbleized sideplates and knob, 2¼ x 1 inches, 4 ounces.

Courtesy Anglers' Club of New York.

H.L. Leonard

c.1880; nickel-silver with black-and-red marbleized sideplates, 3 x ⅞ inches, 5¾ ounces.

Leonard's decorated sideplates were a startling departure from the brass-silver-and-black colorations of most nineteenth-century reels.

Courtesy American Museum of Fly Fishing.

brother Julius developed his father's business into a large-scale manufactory of varied reels under the Vom Hofe mark and for the trade.

Edward Vom Hofe's line of fly reels eventually grew to seven models, including a click reel for trout and bass (the "Peerless"), and an adjustable drag reel for trout and bass (the "Perfection"). Edward was constantly improving his designs, receiving patents in 1879, 1883, 1896, and 1902. His painstaking attention to detail is evident in handcut, countersunk screws, shouldered pillars, sliding oil caps, and the use of Tobin bronze for bearings.

The classic Edward Vom Hofe reel—typically black hard-rubber sideplates with bright nickel-silver frames and S-shaped handles—demonstrates the essence of a style that has had a far-reaching impact on American reel design, traceable to the work of makers such as Otto Zwarg, Arthur Walker, and Stanley Bogdan. In 1940, Vom Hofe's company was sold and moved to Philadelphia, where the Vom Hofe reel continued to be made in a slightly redesigned form. After an interruption due to wartime shortages of materials, the company reopened, then closed for good in 1950.

Julius Vom Hofe

c.1900 (1889 patent); decorative, custom-order trout reel, nickel-silver frame, aluminum spool, hard-rubber sideplates, 2⅜ x ¾ inches, 4 ounces.

Courtesy American Museum of Fly Fishing.

Edward Vom Hofe

c.1890; Peerless trout fly reel, nickel-silver frame, aluminum spool, hard-rubber sideplates, 2⅛ x ¾ inches, 3¼ ounces.

Courtesy American Museum of Fly Fishing.

C.F. Orvis Co.

c.1875 (1874 patent); nickel-silver sideplates and spool,
2⅞ x ½ inches, 4 ounces.

An owner-modified first model. Its numerous perforations and
slim features distinguished this "first popular, modern-style
American fly reel," says Jim Brown in *A Treasury of Reels*.

Courtesy American Museum of Fly Fishing.

Julius Vom Hofe

c.1920; aluminum frame, nickel-silver counterbalanced handle,
hard-rubber sideplates, raised-pillar multiplier, 3⅛ x 1½ inches,
8 ounces.

Courtesy American Museum of Fly Fishing.

Yawman & Erbe Mfg. Co.

c.1912 (1888 patent); aluminum with nickel-plated brass fittings,
automatic fly reel, 3⅜ x 1⅛ inches, 10¾ ounces.

Y&E modified Francis Loomis's 1880 patent and made auto-
matics for thirty years.

Courtesy American Museum of Fly Fishing.

Martin Novelty Works

c.1895; aluminum with nickel-silver trim, side-mounting auto-
matic, 3¼ x ½ inches, 9 ounces. Serial no. 23, one of Martin's first
reels.

From its Ilion, New York (near Utica), origins, the company
became the Martin Reel Company, Mohawk, New York, the
longest-operating reelmaker in the U.S.

Courtesy Catskill Fly Fishing Center.

B.F. Meek & Sons

c.1905; No. 44 nickel-silver single-action, on-off click reel, 2¼ x 1 inches, 6¼ ounces.

The Meek 44 was built from 1899 until about 1911 and is highly treasured by collectors.

Courtesy Anglers' Club of New York.

B.F. Meek & Sons

c.1905; rear of No. 44, with on-off click button, maker's inscription. Serial no. 2853 on foot.

Meek reels were made for over one hundred years (1837–1940).

Courtesy Anglers' Club of New York..

Edward R. Hewitt

c.1945; same specifications as the reel at right, except for an eight-position drag mechanism and 6½-ounce weight. "M.B.A. [Maxine B. Atherton] made by Edward R. Hewitt" engraved on back.

Hewitt made only about twenty reels, all when he was in his eighties, and all for fishing friends. The Maxine Atherton reel is believed to be among the first.

Courtesy American Museum of Fly Fishing.

Edward R. Hewitt

c.1950; aluminum frame, nickel-silver fittings, raised pillars with larger line-roller pillar, fixed click, adjustable seven-position detent drag mechanism, 3½ x ¾ inches, 7 ounces. "Made by Edward R. Hewitt-Ellis C. Newman" engraved on back, and "12" stamped on frame.

Courtesy American Museum of Fly Fishing.

McVickar & Son

*c.1946; aluminum, deep-plum anodized frame, 3 x ⅞ inches,
5½ ounces.*

Harry McVickar, a Tuxedo, New York, angler and shooter,
designed and made the "Bushkill Fly Reel," named after the
Catskill stream where he fished. It featured an innovative ball-
bearing click-drag mechanism along with its classy good looks.

Courtesy American Museum of Fly Fishing.

Art Flick's Hardy Perfect

*c.1945; aluminum with black-leaded finish, nickel-plated-steel ring line
guide, 2⅞ x ⅝ inches, 6 ounces.*

The "Perfect" was introduced about 1890 and has been made almost
continuously ever since, making it one of the most popular reels of
all time.

Courtesy Catskill Fly Fishing Center.

Sparse Grey Hackle's Pflueger Medalist

*c.1930; aluminum with black enamel finish, ring guide,
3¼ x ¾ inches, 3¾ ounces.*

The "Medalist" has been made since 1929. A no-nonsense, practical
fishing tool, it suited Sparse's tastes and those of thousands of
other anglers for more than sixty-five years.

Courtesy Catskill Fly Fishing Center.

Elsie Darbee's Hardy Uniqua

*c.1950; aluminum with black-leaded finish, nickel-silver bar-style
spool latch, 2⅝ x ⅝ inches, 5 ounces.*

The "Uniqua" was made from 1903 to 1958. The near mint condition of Elsie's reel contrasts sharply with that of Sparse's reel,
bearing out the fact that she stayed home at the tying vise while
her husband, Harry, did most of the fishing.

Courtesy Catskill Fly Fishing Center.

Edward R. Hewitt's custom-made cedar flybox, with his favorite Neversink Skaters in the right half of the bottom tray and his patented, stained silkworm-gut leaders just above.
Courtesy American Museum of Fly Fishing.

TWELVE

Flies

~~~~~~~~~~~~~~~~~~~~~~~~~~~

American flytying was very primitive before Theodore Gordon. Robert Barnwell Roosevelt, in his 1884 edition of *The Game Fish of the Northern States and British Provinces*, described the state of American flytying art:

> *Few people in this stage of civilization dress their own trout flies. . . . With the English makers it has always been an especial care that their flies should be dressed well; but here, anything that can be palmed off on an ignorant or indulgent public, or a barbarous country trade, is all that is desired.*

Mary Orvis Marbury, daughter of Charles Frederick Orvis, founder of the Orvis Company, in the 1896 edition of her *Favorite Flies and Their Histories*, echoed Roosevelt, observing that nearly all the tackle dealers in America were Scotch, Irish, or English and that the flies they sold were all imported, thus American anglers used "the flies most favorably known abroad."

Theodore Gordon first learned to make flies when he was thirteen from reading Thaddeus Norris. His skill grew steadily until he became, as it were, a graduate student through his correspondence with and reading the books of Frederic Halford, the great British dry-fly expert.

Hewitt at his fly vise, where he created such famous patterns as his skater, Brown Bivisible, Hardbacked Nymph, and his favorite, the Yellow Stonefly, about which he said, "I can skin the water with this fly if I want to."
Courtesy Anglers' Club of New York.

Eventually, Gordon created many original dry-fly patterns on his own. Some he named, and they survived into modern times; some were nameless and may have been used for only a season. "I fussed after a fly for two years," he wrote, "and named it after a well-known angler," whom he did not identify. There was the Orange Grannom, worked out in 1909, and its close relative the Dark Grannom, "a favorite of mine,

169

also an earlier riser and smaller, that carries a bag of orange colored eggs (dark) at the end of the body."

In many cases, Gordon took the standard American wet-fly patterns and tied them "in dry-fly fashion." The Light Cahill was one of these. The Beaverkill, a wet fly descended from the British Silver Sedge, had been used in this country for about forty years before Gordon picked it up and turned it into a floater.

There was the Gordon, known then as the G.B.S. or Gold Bodied Spinner, which has survived, and of course the Quill Gordon, then called the Gordon Quill, which he tied in a variety of shades and sizes.

Sometime around 1900, Gordon became a professional flytier. He sold his flies mostly by mail, although he had a few friends and customers who got their flies directly from him at his residence or on the stream. They included Abe Snedecor and Dick Robbins of the Brooklyn Fly Fishers, George LaBranche, Guy Jenkins and his father Henry, Willard Spenser, Fred White, and Alfred Caspari.

Whenever **Herman Christian** came to visit Gordon while he was tying flies, Gordon would take the unfinished fly out of the vise and lay it on the table and talk about fishing or something else besides flytying. Said Christian, "He never taught anybody to tie; he never showed anybody anything, not even me." Christian should have known that Gordon did teach one man to tie flies—Roy Steenrod of Liberty. Rube Cross also claimed to have learned under Gordon's tutelage, but on this Christian was adamant: "Gordon never spoke to Rube in his life." So Christian untied and figured out in reverse how Gordon had tied his flies, just as Walt Dette, Harry Darbee, and later generations of Catskill flytiers did in order to learn the professional secrets of the old masters.

One of Gordon's patterns "dissected" by Christian was the Bumble-puppy. It had been designed originally as a bass fly and to use at night for the biggest brown trout. Gordon liked to send one with an order of delicate Quill Gordons and Light Cahills as a startling gift to his

Herman Christian tying a Bumblepuppy.
Courtesy Melvin Eck.

Quill Gordon

(Tied by Theodore Gordon)

Hook: 12 to 16
Tail: Medium blue dun cock hackle fibers
Body: Stripped peacock quill, varnished or
*   wired for strength*
Wings: Wood-duck flank feather
Hackle: Medium blue dun cock hackles

A priceless fly—an original Quill Gordon tied by himself. Note the very sparse hackles, the upright, single-stalk wing, and the compressed wing-and-hackle conformation right behind the eye, all typical of Gordon's dry-fly tying style.

Courtesy Catskill Fly Fishing Center.

Quill Gordon

(Tied by Herman Christian)
Dressing same as above.

Herman Christian's version of the QG. Catskill flytiers after Gordon left a longer, clean "neck" at the expense of a shortened body.

Courtesy Catskill Fly Fishing Center.

Quill Gordon

(Tied by Harry Darbee)
Dressing same as above.

Harry Darbee's version. Christian, Darbee, and later flytiers of the "Catskill School" divided the wood-duck wings.

Courtesy American Museum of Fly Fishing.

customers. Christian changed the pattern slightly and made it even larger, tying it on a 1/0 hook. A Christian Bumblepuppy is credited with a thirteen-pound, four-ounce brown taken by Waldemar Kesk in the Delaware below the mouth of Mongaup River. The trout won a *Field & Stream* national contest.

In the last ten years of Gordon's life, **Roy Steenrod** was probably his closest friend. They fished together often, and Gordon singled him out as his protégé in flytying. Interestingly, in contrast to Herman Christian, Steenrod went on to become the best-known flytying instructor in the Catskills. He taught at the DeBruce conservation camp, at Boy Scout meetings, or anywhere there was a handy vise and materials. He was responsible more than anyone else right after Gordon for passing on the distinctive features of the Catskill style.

Steenrod's biggest claim to flytying fame lies in his having originated one of the all-time favorite brown trout flies in America, the Hendrickson. This pattern was named for his friend and fishing companion A.E. Hendrickson, trucking magnate, backer of rodmaker Jim Payne, and a constant angler on the Beaverkill River.

As recalled by Steenrod, it was the spring of 1916 when he and Hendrickson were fishing at Ferdon's Pool on the lower Beaverkill and encountered a tremendous hatch of the mayfly *Ephemerella subvaria*. At lunchtime, Steenrod tied up some imitations, which were murderously effective. It became their favorite pattern but remained unnamed. Orders from Hendrickson said only, "I need some more of *those flies.*" After several years, Hendrickson finally remarked that the pattern ought to have a name. "All right," said Steenrod, "it's the Hendrickson." In recounting the experience years later to Sparse Grey Hackle, Steenrod said, "I could see that A.E. was pleased."

Whether or not **Rube (Reuben R.) Cross** was taught how to tie by Gordon, he certainly tied his flies in the Gordon manner and, through his book *Tying American Trout Lures* (1936), was a major influence on American flytiers of the thirties and forties. Eugene Connett, fishing writer and owner of Derrydale Press, called Cross "the best professional tier of dry flies in America." He is best known for his Cross Special, Catskill, and Blue Honey Dun patterns.

As good as he was, Rube Cross had to combine a mixture of trades in order to make a living. Besides flytying, he drove a taxi, worked on the town roads, and held the combination job of janitor and bouncer at the Lew Beach dance hall. One night, as recalled by Harry Darbee, "Rube threw Benny Leonard the movie fighter out of the dance hall when Leonard got boisterous; Rube was like a cat on his feet." Another night, he returned home from a dance and found his house in flames, managing to save only a pair of snowshoes. His friends and a group of

Bumblepuppy

(Tied by Herman Christian)

Hook: 1/0 4XL
Tag: Red silk fibers
Body: White silk chenille
Hackle: Red and white hackles
Wings: Brown turkey wing splayed
*   out over white hair*

Christian tied a simplified version of the Bumblepuppy, without Jungle Cock or multi-colored body; a deadly pattern for bass and large brown trout.

Courtesy American Museum of Fly Fishing.

Christian Palmered Wet

(Tied by Herman Christian)

Hook: 4 2XL
Tail: Tan cock hackle fibers
Body: Tan fox-fur dubbing
Hackle: Palmered tan cock hackle
Ribbing: Black thread counterwound
Wings: Wood-duck flank feather, undivided

Christian liked to fish at night with big flies like this one. He caught a 29½-inch, 8-pound, 4-ounce brown in the Neversink on a No. 6 dun fly.

Courtesy Catskill Fly Fishing Center.

Dark Hendrickson

(Tied by Roy Steenrod)

Hook: 10 to 14
Tail: Dark rusty dun cock hackles
Body: Brownish grey fox-fur dubbing
Wing: Wood-duck flank feather
Hackle: Dark rusty dun cock hackles

The dark version of Steenrod's imitation of one of the major fly hatches in the Northeast, and one of the brown trout's favorite morsels.

Courtesy Catskill Fly Fishing Center.

Fanwing Royal Coachman

(Tied by Roy Steenrod)

Hook: 12 to 18
Tail: Golden pheasant tippets
Body: Peacock herl with red floss
*   band in center*
Wing: White mallard or wood-duck breast
*   feathers tied upright and divided*
Hackle: Brown cock hackles

A widely popular fly from the teens through the thirties, when it was displaced by the more durable hairwing coachman. Theodore Gordon tied the first known fanwing coachman and sent it in 1907 to Les Petrie, one of his steady customers, to test. Petrie loved the fanwing style and even had his own version with a yellow silk band in place of the red, which he named the Petrie Royal.

Courtesy Catskill Fly Fishing Center.

Palmered Cahill
(Tied by Rube Cross)
Hook: 12 to 16
Tail: Light ginger cock hackle fibers
Body: Cream fox-fur dubbing
Wing: Wood-duck flank feather, divided
Hackle: Light ginger cock hackles

The Cahill fly originated in England; was modified by Theodore Gordon, who tied a lighter version; then by William Chandler, a former William Mills salesman, who lightened the pattern further to suit his idea of a more effective fly.
Courtesy Catskill Fly Fishing Center.

Wet Spider
(Tied by Rube Cross)
Hook: 12 wet
Tail: Soft dun hackle
Body: Flat gold tinsel
Hackle: Soft dun hackle, sparsely wound

Cross tied his wet flies with wings nearly upright to the hook, like the soft hackles on this spider, "so they can be fished downstream and retrieved with slow short jerks to give them a more natural, life-like action."
Courtesy Catskill Fly Fishing Center.

Nature Fly
(Tied for Louis Rhead)
Hook: 10 1XL
Tail: Extended body
Body: Red silk wound with white thread
Wing and Snoot: Light mallard
Hackle: Ginger cock hackles

Rhead's flies were more creations of his imagination than representations of any actual stream insects; this pattern somewhat resembles the large mayflies.
Courtesy Catskill Fly Fishing Center.

Nature Fly
(Tied for Louis Rhead)
Hook: 10 2XL
Tail: None
Body: Peacock herl (body & head)
Wing: Partridge flank feather
Hackle: Brown cock hackles

This fly is shaped like the old brook trout wet-fly patterns, whose bright colors appealed to *Salvelinus fontinalis*, a species of known gullibility.
Courtesy Catskill Fly Fishing Center.

Whirling Blue Dun

(Attributed to George M.L. LaBranche)

Hook: 12 to 18
Tail: Light blue dun hackle fibers
Body: Muskrat-belly-fur dubbing
Ribbing: Flat gold tinsel
Wing: Light mallard quill segments
Hackle: Light blue dun cock hackles

The W.B.D. was one of LaBranche's favorite flies. There is disagreement over whether he ever tied flies.

Courtesy Catskill Fly Fishing Center.

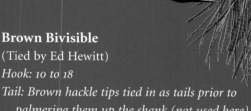

Brown Bivisible

(Tied by Ed Hewitt)

Hook: 10 to 18
Tail: Brown hackle tips tied in as tails prior to
*   palmering them up the shank (not used here)*
Body: Two brown cock hackles palmered at hook
*   bend for two-thirds of shank, then one white*
*   cock hackle palmered up to head*

Ed Hewitt designed this fly to be seen easily by both the trout and the angler.

Courtesy American Museum of Fly Fishing.

Female Beaverkill

(Tied by Mahlon Davidson)

Hook: 12 to 16
Tail: Speckled mallard fibers
Egg Sac: One turn of fine yellow chenille
Body: Blue-grey muskrat-fur dubbing
Wing: Double divided medium grey
*   mallard quill segments*
Hackle: Medium ginger cock hackles

George Cooper, a DeBruce blacksmith and store owner, originated this fly in the late 1890s to represent the female Hendrickson spinner with its yellow egg sac. Davidson bought Cooper's general store and continued his flytying business.

Courtesy Catskill Fly Fishing Center.

Hairwing Royal Coachman

(Tied by Mahlon Davidson)

Hook: 6 to 20
Tail: Golden pheasant tippet strands
Body: In three equal parts: peacock herl,
*   scarlet silk floss, peacock herl*
Wing: White calf-tail hair
Hackle: Red-brown cock hackles

Al McClane credits the hairwing coachman to Rube Cross, who was asked in 1930 to come up with a more durable pattern than the fanwing then in vogue. By the forties, it was hard to find the fanwing version in anyone's fly box.

Courtesy Catskill Fly Fishing Center.

distraught anglers got together and donated clothing, household items, and about fifteen hundred dollars, but he never really recovered from his loss. Shortly after he had reestablished himself farther downstream near the Craigie Clare bridge, conservation officers paid an unexpected visit and fined him for possessing wood-duck and golden pheasant feathers without a license. He developed ulcers and in the early forties moved to Rhode Island, where he supplemented his flytying income by working in a munitions plant and for a realty company.

Ed Hewitt enjoyed experimenting with new fly patterns, but he employed other tiers to make production copies for his fishing and to give to friends. Hewitt was very influential as a fly designer and theorist on the use of his favorite patterns. One of them was a No. 16 Stonefly with yellow body and pheasant wing, about which he remarked: "I find that this is much the best fly for our waters all the time. When I want fish I always put this on, but you must know just how to fish it—wet with a long leader. I can skin the water with this fly if I want to." Hewitt also designed the Brown Bivisible, a palmered brown-and-white fly that both he and the trout could see. This pattern is still very popular today.

It is the Neversink Skater, however, for which Hewitt was best known. This fly is patterned after the butterflies he saw being taken in broad daylight by large leaping trout. It is a No. 16 spider with no tail, tied with extra wide and stiff spade or saddle hackles to make a fly two inches or more in diameter. The fishing method, prescribed by Hewitt, required great casting precision to keep the fly moving on the water, high—and dry—at all times. The moment it got soaked or taken by a fish, Hewitt put on a fresh one.

Walt Dette moved to Roscoe, New York, when he entered the seventh grade and right away took up fly fishing. He and Harry Darbee fished

Elsie and Harry Darbee at their fly vises in the late 1950s.
Courtesy Catskill Fly Fishing Center.

Isonychia Nymph

(Tied by Preston Jennings)

Hook: 10 nymph style

*Tail: Three short pieces of peacock sword
    herl, tied forked*

*Body: Dark claret seal fur and black wool,
    mixed and shredded, then dubbed*

Legs: Grouse feather, one or two turns

A prolific nymph on the Esopus. Jennings gave one to a stranger (a famous magazine editor) at Kahil's Rainbow Lodge in Mount Tremper, telling him to "fish it like a wet fly because it is the only nymph that swims." The man, skeptical at first, caught a dozen trout in the next hour.

Courtesy American Museum of Fly Fishing.

Grey Fox

(Tied by Preston Jennings)

Hook: 10 to 14

Tail: Ginger cock hackle fibers

Body: Light red fox-belly-fur dubbing

Wing: Mallard-drake flank feather

Hackle: One each ginger and grizzly cock hackle

Head: Primrose silk thread

Jennings wrote the first reliable American angling entomology, *A Book of Trout Flies*, in 1935, by matching effective artificials with what was hatching on Catskill streams at the same time. The Grey Fox was one of these patterns.

Courtesy American Museum of Fly Fishing.

A Darbee Hybrid

(Tied by Harry Darbee)

Hook: 12

Tail: Ginger cock hackle fibers

Body: Red fox-belly-fur dubbing

Wing: Double divided mallard wing segments

Hackle: Medium ginger cock hackles

Darbee often tied special patterns to customers' individual tastes. He also sometimes demonstrated tying techniques with whatever materials were lying next to his vise. This hybrid of a Ginger Quill and a Hendrickson could be either.

Courtesy American Museum of Fly Fishing.

Two-Feather Fly

(Tied by Harry Darbee)

Hook: 16 4xs

*Tail, Body, Wing: Spade or back hackle with
    long fibers at tip*

Hackle: Regular dry-fly hackle

Darbee designed this fly for his friend Terrell Moore. The first feather is stroked back to form the forked tail, an elongated body, and wings; the second is wound normally for the hackle, resulting in a large but ultralight fly. It generated lots of excitement in the 1960s, then dropped out of sight.

Courtesy Catskill Fly Fishing Center.

together almost daily in their school years. When he was about twenty, Walt scraped together fifty dollars and offered it to Rube Cross in return for flytying lessons. Cross turned him down, and Walt joined the Catskill line of self-taught flytiers. He began selling flies shortly after his marriage to Winnie Ferdon in 1928, and by 1933 formalized his business as W.C. Dette, Dry Flies, inviting Harry Darbee to join him. The business consisted of Walt, Winnie, Harry, and then Elsie Bivins until 1935, when Harry and Elsie were married and went out on their own as E.B. and H.A. Darbee, Flies and Flytying Supplies.

The Dette flytying tradition continues today in daughter Mary Dette Clark, who learned from her parents their meticulous dry-fly techniques, adding her own Coffin Fly design to the Dette repertory that includes the Corey Ford and the original Coffin Fly design, developed by Walt and Ted Townsend.

In his first year of business, **Harry Darbee** put out a catalog listing 232 patterns, including two new designs he originated "to give us some-

The Darbee tying desks at the Catskill Fly Fishing Center, with everything where it used to be in their home.
Courtesy Catskill Fly Fishing Center.

Neversink Skater

(Tied by Harry Darbee)

Hook: 16 light wire
Hackle: Three extra wide and stiff
  light ginger spade or saddle hackles

Ed Hewitt's signature fly, designed to resemble butterflies he saw being taken in broad daylight by large leaping trout. Darbee saved his biggest hackles for Hewitt to make flies of two inches or more in diameter. Essentially a variant with no tail, it should be fished, said Hewitt, "high and dry."

Courtesy Catskill Fly Fishing Center.

Rat-Faced McDougall

(Tied by Elsie and Harry Darbee)

Hook: 10 to 14
Tail: Ginger cock hackle fibers
Body: Clipped tannish grey deer hair
Wing: Cream grizzly hackle tips
Hackle: Ginger cock hackles

Elsie and Harry Darbee's best-known fly, co-designed with Percy Jennings. It was later modified for Otto von Kienbusch, who, with failing eyesight, asked that a white calf-tail wing be substituted for the hackle tips.

Courtesy Catskill Fly Fishing Center.

Hairwing Royal Coachman

(Tied by Elsie Darbee)

Hook: 6 to 20
Tail: Golden pheasant tippet strands
Body: In three equal parts: peacock herl,
  scarlet silk floss, peacock herl
Wing: White calf-tail hair
Hackle: Red-brown cock hackles

In addition to the Rube Cross credit for designing this fly, there is also a reference to its creation by Charles F. Orvis, though not as well substantiated. Orvis or Cross—take your pick—it is still a great fly.

Courtesy Judie Darbee Vinciguerra.

Coffin Fly

(Tied by Elsie Darbee)

Hook: 8 to 12 3XL
Tail: Black bear hair or cock hackle fibers
Body: Clipped white deer hair
Wing: Black cock hackle tips
Hackle: Two or three badger cock hackles

This fly was developed in 1929 by Walt Dette and Ted Townsend to imitate the Green Drake spinner, a big, sexy fly and trout favorite of early June.

Courtesy Judie Darbee Vinciguerra.

The Dette flytying tradition continues in its seventh decade in the skilled hands of Mary Dette Clark.

Courtesy Catskill Fly Fishing Center, montage by Enrico Ferorelli.

Henryville Special

(Tied by Walt Dette)

Hook: 10 to 16
Body: Olive silk floss
Ribbing: Grizzly hackle palmered
Underwing: Wood-duck flank fibers
Wing: Mallard wing quill segments,
  tied on flaring outward
Hackle: Brown cock hackle

Originated as the Henryville by Pennsylvania flytier Hiram Brobst with a scarlet silk body, altered by Ernest Schwiebert to currently preferred green silk body, a successful all-round caddis imitation.

Courtesy Catskill Fly Fishing Center.

Delaware Adams

(Tied by Walt Dette)

Hook: 10 to 16
Tail: Grizzly hackle fibers
Body: Medium olive wool or fur dubbing
Ribbing: Palmered grizzly hackle
Wing: Grizzly hackle tips
Hackle: Mixed grizzly and brown cock hackles

A Dette original, combining features of the Henryville Special with the Adams, this one tied by Walt on Opening Day 1989. He designed the fly in the sixties when the Delaware's two dams had just extended the trout zone and generated increased angling interest in both branches and the main river.

Courtesy Catskill Fly Fishing Center.

Light Cahill

(Tied by Winnie Dette)

Hook: 12 to 14
Tail: Pale ginger cock hackle fibers
Body: Cream-colored fox-fur dubbing
Wing: Wood-duck or mandarin drake flank feather
Hackle: Pale ginger cock hackles

Art Flick said this was "probably the one dry fly that all fishermen carry" and included it in his *Streamside Guide to Naturals and Their Imitations*.

Courtesy Catskill Fly Fishing Center.

Coffin Fly

(Tied by Mary Dette Clark)

Hook: 10 to 12 2XL
Tail: Three peccary bristles, splayed
Underbody: White poly yarn
Body: White saddle hackle, trimmed close to body
Ribbing: 3/0 white thread
Wing: Teal flank, divided
Hackle: Four golden badger hackles,
  black centers

The actual story on this fly is that Walt's friend Ted Townsend had just come from a funeral when they sat down at the vise and began tying a new pattern for the spinner of the Green Drake. In a moment of funereal wit, in keeping with its black-and-white austerity, they named it the Coffin Fly.

Courtesy Catskill Fly Fishing Center.

thing special to offer our customers." One of them, "H.A. Darbee's Mid-Summer Special," was a tiny fly made only from hackle-tip wings, palmered bare hook shank, and tail—all feathers of the same bird. Said Darbee in the catalog, "These flies will take any rising fish nine times out of ten when correctly presented."

The other fly he called "H.A. Darbee's Special Mayfly." It was conceived as a hybrid of the deer-hair bassbug and a large trout fly, and indeed came to be known as the Beaverkill Bastard, to be fished when the big mays and drakes were on the water. It was tied on a No. 10 3XL hook, and had three hackles, a clipped deer-hair body, and double hackle-point wings. Percy Jennings, one of the Darbees' customers, tied it smaller and renamed it the Rat-Faced McDougall, turning it into one of the best all-round trout flies to come out of the Catskills. It went through one more evolution when another Darbee customer, Otto von Kienbusch, requested that the wings be changed to white hair so he could see the fly with his failing eyes. With this change, the pattern stabilized and the Rat-Faced McDougall became a staple of the Darbees' business. Said Harry, "I cranked out the bodies, Elsie trimmed them to shape, and either of us winged and hackled them. It was the only way we could turn out such a fussy pattern and price it competitively."

Other patterns developed by Darbee include the Shad Fly, an early-spring caddis imitation, and the Spate Fly, a large, dark salmon fly to be fished in high, discolored water.

When **Art Flick** came to Schoharie Creek in 1934, the valley had no fly-fishing professionals. In order to succeed as an innkeeper catering to

Winnie Dette tying flies at the 1936 Sportsmen's Show held at the Grand Central Palace in New York City. [Flies on the opposite page and page 185, except for Walt's Dace, were tied in 1930 by either Walt or Winnie for a framed display that traveled the country in an advertising campaign for the liquor distributor Gallagher & Burton.]

Courtesy Mary Dette Clark.

Pink Lady

(Tied by the Dettes; see note
in caption at left)
Hook: 12 to 16
Tail: Dark ginger hackle fibers
Body: Pink silk floss
Ribbing: Fine flat gold tinsel
Wing: Light grey duck wing segments, double divided
Hackle: Ginger cock hackles

George LaBranche's celebrated fly. As Rube Cross observed
in the 1930s, "Today when an angler orders Pink Ladies he
invariably means the LaBranche Pink Lady, a palmer-tied fly
of bivisible effect." (The Beaverkill below is tied palmer.)

Courtesy Catskill Fly Fishing Center.

Ginger Quill

(Tied by the Dettes)
Hook: 10 to 16
Tail: Golden ginger cock hackle fibers
Body: Stripped peacock quill
Wing: Slate mallard wing quill segments, double divided
Hackle: Golden ginger cock hackles

Frederic Halford has the first mention of the GQ in his
Floating Flies and How to Dress Them (1886). He sent it and
forty-nine other flies in the famous 1890 letter to Theodore
Gordon, who redressed it in the Catskill style. It has been an
extremely versatile American pattern ever since.

Courtesy Catskill Fly Fishing Center.

Beaverkill

(Tied by the Dettes)
Hook: 12 to 16
Tail: Brown hackle fibers
Body: White silk floss
Ribbing: Brown cock hackle, palmered
Wing: Medium grey mallard wing quill segments,
* double divided*
Hackle: Brown cock hackles

This fly began as a British wet pattern (the Silver Sedge), was
renamed around 1850 (still wet) by Judge Fitz-James Fitch
after his favorite trout stream, and then was turned into a dry
fly in the 1890s by Theodore Gordon.

Courtesy Catskill Fly Fishing Center.

Gordon

(Tied by the Dettes)
Hook: 12 to 18
Tail: Badger hackle fibers
Body: Golden silk floss
Ribbing: Fine gold oval tinsel
Wing: Wood-duck flank feather
Hackle: Light cream badger hackles,
* grey centers*

Originally known as the G.B.S. or Golden Bodied Spinner,
this fly was created by Theodore Gordon.

Courtesy Catskill Fly Fishing Center.

fly fishermen, he also had to become a guide and a flytier. His first teacher in flytying was Clarence Banks, a half-Indian hunter and fisherman who lived on the stream above Lexington. Ray Bergman came up from Nyack, and he too helped Flick with his flies. It was Preston Jennings, though, who introduced Flick to natural dun hackles, judged his tying efforts, and cheered him on to become a flytier of extraordinary capability. Jennings himself was responsible for creating the American March Brown from its English counterpart, and for the Grey Fox Variant.

Because Art Flick never tied on a commercial scale, few fishermen besides his Westkill Tavern guests could buy flies from him. "Dana Lamb could get flies out of him when nobody else could," recalled Sparse Grey Hackle. "I remember the night Dana's fishing vest was stolen down in the Antrim Lodge bar, off of a coat hook. They got his fly boxes and everything, but the only thing he wept about to me was his Flick flies."

Flick originated the Red Quill to imitate the male *Ephemerella subvaria*. Roy Steenrod had matched the females about twenty years earlier with his Hendrickson. The dressings of these two flies are identical except for their bodies. "I had such success with this fly," said Art, "that I decided to put my same old favorite red quill on Jennings's Blue Variant, Gold Body." The result was Flick's Dun Variant, a killer fly during the *Isonychia* hatch. He also modified Jennings's Grey Fox Variant body from a gold tinsel to a ginger quill, and it became the continuing favorite among the fishermen at Westkill Tavern. Flick liked quill bodies because they were quicker to tie, more durable, and easier to keep dry while fishing. Other patterns developed by Flick include the Black-Nose Dace bucktail and the Hendrickson nymph.

Many other flies were originated and fished in the Catskills. Some passed on with their creators; some were adopted more widely and are fished on the rivers today. George Cooper, a local blacksmith and storekeeper, originated the Female Beaverkill; when he first tied it in the 1890s, it was known as the "Nice Nelly." Scotty Conover of the Brooklyn Fly Fishers created the enduring Conover in the 1920s. Mahlon Davidson, of Lew Beach and then DeBruce, tied a fly similar to the Light Cahill with a fox-fur body dyed pale green with willow bark, called the Davidson Special. Other Catskill patterns include the Spent Wing Woodruff, Neversink, Catskill, Bradley Special, Campbell's Fancy, Murray's Favorite, Christian Special, Petrie's Green Egg Sac, Quack Special, and Pink Lady.

Two grizzly roosters: *Frank Kuttner's letting loose in the hands of its respectful owner; and Dave Catizone's on the patch he designed for his flytying guild, which has members from eleven states who are perpetuating the Catskill tying tradition.*
Courtesy Judie Darbee Vinciguerra and the Catskill Fly Tyers Guild.

Conover

(Tied by the Dettes)

Hook: 12 to 16
Tail: Cream hackle fibers
Body: 2/3 rabbit fur, 1/3 red wool mixed
*   to get distinct reddish dubbing*
Wing: None
Hackle: Cream badger hackles, brown centers

Scotty Conover of the Fly Fishers Club of Brooklyn created this enduring pattern in the 1920s. A staunch dry-fly man, he once told Sparse Grey Hackle that he had not fished a wet fly in over thirty years.

Courtesy Catskill Fly Fishing Center.

Corey Ford

(Tied by the Dettes)

Hook: 12 to 16
Tail: Light ginger cock hackle fibers
Body: Very light green fox- or rabbit-fur dubbing
Wing: Medium dun hackle points
Hackle: Light ginger cock hackles

Corey Ford, a New York fishing writer, often stayed at the River View Inn, where he met and became a close friend of the Dettes. Ford loved Barnhart's Pool, so Walt tied this pattern for him to use there.

Courtesy Catskill Fly Fishing Center.

Walt's Dace

(Tied by Walt Dette)

Hook: 6 to 10 3XL
Underbody: Embroidery cotton or floss, tied heavy
Body: Medium flat silver tinsel
Ribbing: Fine oval silver tinsel
Throat: Yellow, then white, bucktail strands tied under hook
*   extending one-half shank length beyond hook*
Wing: Brown bucktail, then four dun-dyed badger
*   hackles extending same as throat hairs*
Head: Black lacquered

This fly is named not for Dette but for his friend Walt Maus, who first used it to pull a twenty-four-inch, four-pound brown out of Junction Pool in the 1920s.

Courtesy Catskill Fly Fishing Center.

Petrie's Green Egg Sac

(Tied by the Dettes)

Hook: 12 to 18
Tail: Dun cock hackle fibers
Body: Dark muskrat-fur dubbing
Egg Sac: Green wool or fine chenille
Wing: Wood-duck flank feather, divided
Hackle: Dun cock hackles

Les Petrie, manager of the old Ansonia Hotel in New York City, was an inveterate angler and innovative flytier. He devised this pattern to imitate an early-season caddis, though it is tied in the mayfly style.

Courtesy Catskill Fly Fishing Center.

Art Flick memorabilia: his vise, cigar boxes, tying tools, and the first edition of his pathbreaking book, Streamside Guide.

Courtesy Catskill Fly Fishing Center, montage by Enrico Ferorelli.

March Brown

(Tied by Art Flick)

Hook: 10 to 12
Tail: Ginger cock hackle fibers
Body: Greyish yellow-brown fox-fur dubbing
Wing: Mandarin drake brownish flank feather,
*   with distinct barring, divided*
Hackle: Dark grizzly and dark ginger wound together
Head: Orange silk

Preston Jennings created the American March Brown from its English counterpart for the hatch that emerges right after the Quill Gordons and Hendricksons. "Being a large and meaty morsel...it is the first really large fly of the season...it appeals to trout of all sizes," wrote Flick in his *Streamside Guide*.

Courtesy American Museum of Fly Fishing.

Red Quill

(Tied by Art Flick)

Hook: 12
Tail: Dun cock hackle fibers
Body: Rhode Island Red cock hackle quill,
*   well soaked prior to winding onto hook,*
*   and lacquered to hold in place*
Wing: Mandarin or wood-duck drake flank feather
Hackle: Medium dun cock hackles

A Flick-designed fly, tied to represent the male of the hatch matched by Steenrod's Hendrickson. As Flick observed, "The male will emerge on one riffle, the female on another," and his experiments proved you had to have the right one on or go virtually fishless.

Courtesy Catskill Fly Fishing Center.

Cream Variant

(Tied by Art Flick)

Hook: 12 short shank
Tail: Cream cock hackle fibers
Body: Cream cock's quill, well soaked and
*   lacquered as with the Red Quill*
Hackle: Two to three cream cock hackles,
*   several sizes larger in relation to hook,*
*   wound tightly together*

This pattern matches the *Potamanthus distinctus*, a late-season fly that emerges in the evenings, usually in quiet water, all very convenient for the angler, as the natural is easy to identify and the fly easy to see.

Courtesy Judie Darbee Vinciguerra.

Dun Variant

(Tied by Art Flick)

Hook: 10 to 12 short shank
Tail: Dun cock hackle fibers
Body: Rhode Island Red cock's hackle quill,
*   stripped, soaked, wound, and lacquered*
Hackle: Two to three dark dun cock hackles,
*   several sizes larger in relation to hook,*
*   wound tightly together*

Flick modified Preston Jennings's Blue Variant, Gold Body, by putting his favorite red quill on it, creating Flick's Dun Variant, a killer fly during the *Isonychia bicolor* hatch.

Courtesy Catskill Fly Fishing Center.

"Except for the small space around the customer's feet, Deren's shop is three hundred and sixty degrees of fishing equipment, camping equipment, books, and uncategorizable stuff."—Ian Frazier, The New Yorker, April 19, 1982.
Photograph by Larry Robins.

The sign on the door at Jim Deren's Angler's Roost in the Chrysler Building, one of three locations in Manhattan's east forties where he tied and sold flies, dispensed wisdom, and attended all comers for some four decades. "We don't sell anybody," he said. "We advise, and then they do their own buying." I know, I listened to his advice and bought lots of stuff from him in my first years as a fly fisher.
Photograph by Ed Pfizenmaier.

Grey Fox Variant

(Tied by Preston Jennings)

Hook: 10 to 14
Tail: Ginger cock hackle fibers
Body: Flat gold tinsel
Hackle: Ginger cock and grizzly cock hackles,
*   mixed, several sizes larger in relation to*
*   hook, tightly wound*

Inspired by the variants of Dr. William Baigent of Yorkshire, England, Jennings tied his own "flies of the long hackle type," in this case modifying the Grey Fox to create a fly "which lands on the water with a minimum of fuss."

Courtesy Catskill Fly Fishing Center.

Grey Fox Variant

(Tied by Art Flick)

Hook: 10 to 12
Tail: Ginger cock hackle fibers
Body: Light ginger or cream cock hackle quill,
*   stripped, soaked, wound, and lacquered*
Hackle: Light ginger, dark ginger, and grizzly
*   cock hackles, "wound over each other and*
*   bunched as much as possible"*

In six years of keeping a fly inventory at the Westkill Tavern, Flick found the GFV to be twice as popular as the second and third favorites (Dun Variant and Quill Gordon). He modified Jennings's pattern with his preferred quill body and tied it to imitate the Green Drake.

Courtesy Catskill Fly Fishing Center.

Hare's Ear Wet Fly

(Tied by Art Flick)

Hook: 6 to 16 wet
Tail: Brown cock hackle fibers
Body: Hare's ear (or mask) fur dubbing
Ribbing: Fine flat gold tinsel
Wing: Light to medium grey duck quill segments
Hackle: Dubbing picked out at throat to
*   represent legs*

Hare's ear wets and nymphs, based on an old English pattern, are ubiquitous early-season "sunk" flies. Most Catskill flytiers, and anglers, have favorite versions of the Hare's Ear.

Courtesy Judie Darbee Vinciguerra.

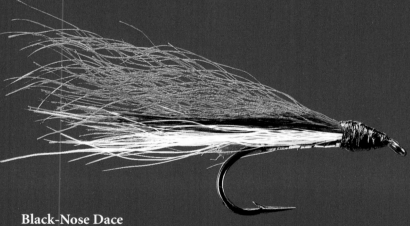

Black-Nose Dace

(Tied by Art Flick)

Hook: 4 to 10 3XL
Tag: Red yarn, very short
Body: Medium silver flat tinsel
Wing: In sequence: polar bear, black bear,
*   brown bucktail*
Head: Black lacquered

Flick created this pattern after the minnow he found most often in fishes' stomachs. White bucktail and black skunk tail may be used in place of polar and black bear hair. Flick tied the white and brown hair at twice the shank length and the black hair slightly shorter to represent the minnow's side stripe.

Courtesy American Museum of Fly Fishing.

Harry Darbee, holding one of his prized
Blue Andalusian roosters, source of his
coveted natural dun hackles. He started at
age ten "raising chickens to get a feather to
tie a fly to catch a fish," and became as well
known for his flock of dun chickens as he
and Elsie were for their flies.
Photograph by Larry Robins.

White Wulff

(Tied by Lee Wulff)

Hook: 10 to 16
*Tail: White calf-body hair (body fibers are
    straighter than calf-tail fibers), divided*
Body: Cream wool or Angora rabbit-fur dubbing
Wing: White calf-body hair, divided
Hackle: Silver badger cock hackles

While in his mid-twenties and fishing in the Northeast, Lee Wulff developed his Wulff series, flies that substituted hair for feathers in the wing and tail, thus achieving greater floatability and durability. The White Wulff, his take on the Coffin Fly, is great just at dark—the larger fish respond to its fat presence, and the angler has a few more minutes to see his fly.

Courtesy Catskill Fly Fishing Center.

Royal Wulff

(Tied by Lee Wulff)

Hook: 10 to 16
Tail: Brown bucktail-hair fibers
*Body: In three equal parts: peacock herl,
    scarlet silk floss, peacock herl*
Wing: White calf-body hair, divided
Hackle: Brown cock hackles

"I wanted a buggier-looking, heavier-bodied fly . . . and I came up with bucktail . . . the first use of animal hair on dry flies. The Royal Wulff made the old, difficult-to-float, but beautiful, Royal Coachman pattern into a hell of a fly."—from *Lee Wulff on Flies*.

Courtesy Catskill Fly Fishing Center.

Female Beaverkill Wet

(Tied by Sid Duncan)

Hook: 12 to 18
Tail: Grey mallard flank fibers
Egg Sac: Fine yellow chenille, one turn
Body: Blue-grey muskrat-fur dubbing
Wing: Medium grey mallard quill segments
Hackle: Medium ginger or red-brown hen hackles

Duncan was a commercial flytier from the 1930s to the 1950s, based in the Neversink valley.

Courtesy Catskill Fly Fishing Center.

Able Mabel

(Tied by Ed Van Put)

Hook: 12 to 16
Tail: Dark to chocolate brown hackle fibers
Body: Mink-underfur dubbing with a few guardhairs left in
Ribbing: Amber cotton thread
Wing: Wood-duck flank fibers, divided
Hackle: Red-brown and grizzly cock hackles mixed

The Woman Flyfishers Club commissioned this fly in honor of Mabel Ingalls, one of their earliest members. Van Put styled it in the classic Catskill manner, choosing a mink body as suited to Mabel's panache and heritage as J.P. Morgan's granddaughter.

From the author's private stock.

PART THREE

Heritage

Fisherman in the Wilderness.
Daniel Huntington, oil on canvas, 1855.
© 1999 Christie's Images, Inc.

THIRTEEN

Early Catskill Fly Fishers

(Above) Title page from the 1933 privately published edition of Washington Irving's essay "The Angler," which originally appeared in 1819 in The Sketch Book of Geoffrey Crayon, Gent.
Courtesy Anglers' Club of New York.

(Left) Judge Fitz-James Fitch, in an 1883 photo, securely harnessed to his commodious basket. He lived in Prattsville, maintained law offices at 7 Warren Street in New York City, and fished often on the upper Neversink with a group of doctors calling themselves the "Fishicians."
Courtesy A.N. Cheney Collection.

Fly fishing in America, as in England, grew out of the Industrial Revolution. And, as American industrialization trailed England's by a good half century, so did our coming of age as anglers. Before 1850, in keeping with an agricultural economy, most fishing in the United States was done not for recreation but for subsistence.

Soon after the Civil War, with the effects of industrialization accelerating in American society, big cities got dirtier, noisier, and more crowded. Significantly, they were also the source of increasing wealth and leisure to escape these harassments. Getting out of the city and back to nature became the ideal pastime for millions of urban Americans. They flocked to the country for long summer vacations, and eventually —when transportation improved—for weekends. They were the guests at the countless hotels and boardinghouses that sprang up in the late 1800s in the Catskills and other accessible "wilderness" regions. Their pastimes included hiking, picnicking, porch sitting, vista viewing, and— for the more adventuresome—hunting and fishing.

Fly fishing gained momentum as newly monied urban industrialists, using English angling techniques and equipment, spread out from Boston, New York, and Philadelphia to the lakes and streams of Maine, the Adirondacks, the Poconos, the Catskills, and Long Island.

Even before this trend—and among the earliest of American fly fishers—**Washington Irving** returned from England, "completely bitten with the angling mania." In his essay "The Angler," contained in *The Sketch Book of Geoffrey Crayon, Gent.*, published in 1819, he describes an outing he and a group of friends took on a brook that drains the eastern slopes of the Catskills:

It was early in the year; but as soon as the weather was auspicious and that the spring began to melt into the verge of summer, we took rod in hand and sallied into the country, as stark mad as was even Don Quixote from reading books of chivalry.

Robert Barnwell Roosevelt (at right) at
Peekamoose on upper Rondout Creek.
Author of Game Fish of the Northern
States of America and British Provinces
(1862), Roosevelt was appointed one of the
three commissioners of the New York State
Fisheries Commission when it was founded
in 1868.

Courtesy A.N. Cheney Collection.

One of our party had equalled the Don in the fulness of his equip-
ments, being attired cap-a-pie for the enterprise. He wore a broad-
skirted fustian coat perplexed with half a hundred pockets, a pair of
stout shoes and leathern gaiters, a basket slung on one side for fish, a
patent rod, a landing net, and a score of other inconveniences only to be
found in the true angler's armory. Thus harnessed for the field, he was
as great a matter of stare and wonderment among the country folk,
who had never seen a regular angler, as was the steel-clad hero of La
Mancha among the goatherds of the Sierra Morena.

"Regular anglers" in America were sparse in the early 1800s, as were
the writings of their whereabouts. In August of 1838, *The American Turf
Register and Sporting Magazine* published this report on fishing near
New York:

The largest proportion [of anglers] are whipping their flies over the
placid ponds of Long Island, where the run of trout this season is of
unusually fine size. Two or three parties, made up principally of "old
hands," have lately made a descent upon the rivers of Sullivan and
Montgomery counties, in this state, and with immense success. The
Williewemauk, Calikoon, and Beaver-kill, are three of the finest trout
streams in this country; they are comparatively unknown to city
anglers, and are less fished than any others of like pretensions within
our knowledge. The trout are large, very numerous, and of the most
delicious flavour.

As the Spring of 1865, approached, those Members of the club of **Fishicians** who were located in New York, had several informal meetings, and there was much correspondence between them, and other members dwelling in provincial towns. The Corresponding Secretary, also, scattered many letters broadcast over the land, in which were propounded many questions, all looking towards the Streams of Maine as the ground for the next Campaign —
But the club finally abandoned the trip to Maine, when they learned that, Trout do not take the fly in those waters until the middle of June, They relinquished the idea of Going to Maine with the less reluctance, that a trip so far from rail-roads, and telegraphs presented some objections to those of the party who were men of family, and then, there were others whose health and tempers would have suffered from so long a post-ponement of the Spring fishing —
The Corresponding Secretary, therefore, laid up his elaborate

---

enemy's works."
Accordingly Admiral Adams, with his flag-ship the Mary Powell, having on board the supply train, and the handsome stores of the U.S.S Commission, executed a rapid flank movement on Rondout, which he took on the afternoon of Saturday, May 20th — A proud moment this for the Admiral — It was not the first time he had burned powder on this very ground. The screeching of his band . . . shells and the blare of . . . his bugle! had been . . . heard them before, . . . and his was there . . . had welcomed "Morning . . . the notes of . . . Having . . . "call" . . . town under . . . placed the and confiscated . . . Martial law marched rapidly on Kingston — an Omnibus, he The behavior of the troops was excellent, no pillaging was permitted, and the inhabitants in several instances, came to their windows in crowds of twos and threes. Kingston surrendered without firing a gun

5

While writing the above the Secretary sitteth before a cheerful grate, in his pleasant room, at the Alms House, in the brown, Nutfalling Month of October, Well nourished and somnolent he can scarcely believe that he was ever cold and wet, and taking the pipe from his lips he saith, "Pleasant is it from the Shore to see the Mariners tossing upon the brine!" — It was about this time that the donor confessed that his . . . name was Widdle — Afraid! all the confusion, the Secretary . . . has the satisfaction of believing . . . he assisted . . . tying one . . . horses. He . . . prefers never . . . who put . . . boxes in the . . . the floor, as he has at present . . . the kindest feelings towards every member of the club. After caring for the animals the association directed its efforts toward its own comfort. The North East corner of the barn was

15.

---

fallen across the stream, or on the meadow not white with strawberry blossoms, with moss tufted bogs for seats. Emphatically, the . . . best part of lunch in the desert . . . Having satisfied your animal . . . cravings, you fit yourself . . . in between several . . . soft rocks resting . . . your head upon one . . . of them, and while . . . indolently — puffing a . . . fragrant cloud you recount to each other the details of the morning and discuss each other's theories of flies and fish — Then rising with renewed hopes, you take up your rod, disentangling your fly from its chance adhesions, and wading out into the deepest water, without a shiver, you begin the contest between skill and cunning — This was a beautiful day and the stream was in

42 —

Pages from the outing journal of the "Fishicians," a small group of anglers—mostly doctors from New York and "provincial towns"—whose excursion to the Neversink River in 1865 was detailed by their "Secretary," Walter DeForest Day, with illustrations by fellow member Dr. Otis. In ten days of fishing, they caught 1,535 brook trout, none heavier than a pound.
Courtesy American Museum of Fly Fishing.

The success of city anglers was not lost on their country cousins. In
the first American book about fishing, *The American Angler's Guide*
(1845), author John Brown reported that "the scientific and graceful art
of throwing the artificial fly" was not so difficult as generally imagined,
for he had seen such "untutored examples" as the raftsmen and lumber-
men from the Delaware River in the fishing tackle stores of New York
"selecting with the eyes of professors and connoisseurs the red, black,
and grey hackle flies, which they use with astonishing dexterity on the
wooded streams of their mountain homes."

Robert Barnwell Roosevelt, a socially prominent New York lawyer,
writer, and pioneering angler, wrote one of the early American fishing
books, *Game Fish of the Northern States of America and British Provinces*
(1862), in which he observed the changes that were taking place in sport
fishing of the day:

> *The brooks of Long Island, especially on the southern shore, abound
> with trout. But they are few in comparison with the hordes that once*

swarmed in the streams of Sullivan and Orange counties, and in fact
all the lower tier of counties in this State, before 1851 when the Erie
Railroad was built, and opened the land to the crowd of market men.
. . . No one wanted to travel beyond Sullivan County [home of the
Beaverkill, Willowemoc, and Neversink rivers]; the best shooting and
fishing in the world was to be found there.

When the railroad was first opened, the country was literally
overrun, and [local rivers], even Beaver Kill, which we thought inex-
haustible, were fished out. For many years trout had almost ceased
from out of the waters, but the horrible public, having their attention
drawn to the Adirondacks, gave it a little rest, and now the fishing
is good.

Once the Catskill streams were discovered as "boss places for trout fishing," their proximity to the largest metropolis and the arrival of rail transportation attracted thousands of aspiring Waltons into this paradise of trouting. The Catskills became, in the words of one outdoor writer, "the merry stamping ground for those whose wont it is during the heated term to shake the dust of business from their shoes and change the rappings of the 'ticker' for the clickings of the reel."

The best-known American fly fisherman of the nineteenth century was **Thaddeus Norris,** author of *The American Angler's Book*. John McDonald said of Norris: "He knew about everything there was to know in his time, put it all down in 1864, and thereby established the school of early American fly fishing with a rounded theory and practice."

Norris fished extensively in the Catskills. One of his favorite places to start from was the Boscobel, a hotel in Westfield Flats, now Roscoe, not far from famous Junction Pool, where the Beaverkill and Willowemoc meet. The Boscobel was owned by Harry Darbee's great uncle, Chester Darbee. Norris dedicated his book to "the little club of Houseless Anglers," a small group of friends organized around 1852, including himself and Chester Darbee, who fished mainly on the Beaverkill and neighboring streams. In describing the club, Norris said, "All the members (their number never exceeded ten) were fly-fishers, some of whom had met for the first time on the stream and had become acquainted without any conventional introduction. We chose the unassuming name of the 'Houseless Anglers' in contradistinction to the old Fish-House clubs—associations rather of a convivial tendency than that of pure angling."

In a sense, women can be credited with greater spunk than men as pioneer fly fishers; it took considerable courage for them to wade into male-dominated streams of the late 1800s and try their skills as fly casters. Interestingly, Sparse Grey Hackle credits the dry fly with luring women onto the stream, noting that the coming of the dry fly into

One of two known fishing photographs taken of Theodore Gordon, with an unnamed woman—his "best chum" in fishing—believed to be in front of Chandler's boardinghouse a few hundred feet above the old Neversink bridge.

general popularity coincides approximately with the coming of the woman angler. Indeed, he advances the theory that "dry-fly fishing is more a woman's than a man's game," in that women are often better in dexterity, coordination, reflexes, sensitive touch, keen eyesight, and close concentration—all attributes of the accomplished dry-fly fisher.

Theodore Gordon's "best chum" in fishing was a woman. "She tramped just as hard and fished quite as patiently as any man I ever knew," he said. She wore a tam-o-shanter, sweater, short jacket, and skirts, with stout shoes and leggings, and waded, as did Gordon, without waterproofs. We never learned her name, only that she was a visitor around 1895 in the Catskills. By the time Gordon met other fishing friends on the Neversink, she had left him—"very much disappointed in love," said Herman Christian.

Gordon welcomed the entry of women into an almost exclusively male sport. It surprised him that more women did not go fishing, noting that they were usually great enthusiasts when they did. He admired the modern sporting woman:

> *The ideal heroine nowadays is far removed from the wasp-waisted, die-away creature of the early portion of the [1800s]. The girl of the twentieth century is a fine upstanding woman, with a flat back, large frame, and the limbs of a Juno.*

Fred White, who began fishing at Jay Davidson's Trout Valley Farm

(Top) Mrs. Robert Barnwell Roosevelt,
around 1890, fishing at Peekamoose, in
proper attire for a lady fly fisher of that day,
using a long rod, open-fingered gloves, and
what appears to be a sidemount reel.
Courtesy A.N. Cheney Collection.

(Bottom) Fred White's pioneering woman
angler, circa 1895, who dared "to brave the
disapproval of the porch sitters" at Davidson's
Trout Valley Farm, shown here fishing below
the Beaverkill covered bridge.
Courtesy Anglers' Club of New York Bulletin.

on the upper Beaverkill at about
the same time Gordon was
escorting his best chum around
the Neversink, witnessed the
emergence of women anglers. In
the Anglers' Club of New York
Bulletin of 1923, he wrote:
I remember distinctly the first
woman at Beaverkill to put on
boots and, even with a knee length
skirt, dare to brave the disapproval
of the porch sitters at Davidson's.
It simply wasn't done and she
came pretty near being regarded
as fast as the water that rippled
about her knees. Now the river is full of 'em and they don't bother with
skirts either. And they catch fish—some of them—and big ones, too.

Whether you like it or not the women are here to stay in trout fishing . . . and when all is said and done, I believe it to be an excellent
thing—for the women. They can wear my second best waders any time.

FOURTEEN

Theodore Gordon

~~~~~~~~~~~~~~~~~~~~~~~~~~~~~~

With gratitude and acknowledgment to John McDonald.

In an accident of history, both the modern dry fly and the brown trout were brought to America at the same time, creating a double revolution. Trying to catch a brown trout with a dry fly on the rivers of the Catskills was the beginning of the art of dry-fly fishing as we know it in this country. Theodore Gordon—with his pioneering experiments, discoveries, and reporting—was the key figure in bringing about this new era.

Gordon was born of a well-to-do family in Pittsburgh in 1854. Fly fishing from the age of fourteen, he lived a remarkable life, almost non-existent in our day. A man of taste and intelligence, a restrained yet warm and exciting fishing writer, Gordon fled civilization for a retreat on the Neversink River. He put one thing only into his mind—the stream—and sustained it there unflaggingly for a great many years. An inexplicable performance, probably never to be duplicated.

Gordon's rare dedication to the sport came about by virtue of an illness that barred him from the life of a stockbroker or other conventional calling and kept him in the mountains. That at any rate was his excuse for giving his good mind exclusively for many years to the subject of fly fishing. He spit blood during his last three years and died, May 1, 1915, of tuberculosis. What we really know of him is that he lived a sweet, good life, perhaps the only man ever to express with his whole life the ideal of the anglers' brotherhood.

Theodore Gordon was one of the first to recognize and promote the virtues of brown trout. Looking back over the marvelous fishing he had had since his first brown in 1889, Gordon wrote in 1903:

Fifteen years ago, in many of our best New York trout streams, a one-pound native trout was a big fish. In all my experiences of waters easily accessible from New York, I took but one fish of sixteen inches. Since the introduction of the brown trout, all this is changed. The average size of trout taken has much increased, and many fish of two pounds are caught every season with fly. Not only is this the case, but not a year passes that

Gordon memorabilia: envelopes from England containing feathers he ordered for his flytying; a fishing photograph; the Trout Valley Farm register signed by him and his mother, Fanny, on June 26, 1906; a letter signed by him; and a Quill Gordon fly tied by him (can you find it?).
Courtesy Catskill Fly Fishing Center, montage by Enrico Ferorelli.

a number of immense fish are not hooked by fly fishermen. I mean fish weighing from four to six pounds. These usually escape, owing to the light tackle used, but they afford a man a sensation that he is in no danger of forgetting to the last day of his life.

The first mention of "dry" fly fishing in America appeared in 1864 in Thad Norris's *The American Angler's Book*. Norris was fishing with a friend on Willowemoc Creek, the fish were "shy," and his friend "put on a Grannom for a stretcher, and a minute Jenny Spinner for a dropper. . . . By cracking the moisture from them between each throw, he would lay them so lightly on the glassy surface that a brace of Trout would take them at almost every cast, before they sank down or were drawn away. . . . Here was an exemplification of the advantage of keeping one's flies dry."

Theodore Gordon had prepared himself for the coming of the dry fly. He had grown up with *The American Angler's Book* (his "book of books"), and from it he had learned to face upstream and fish his wet flies dry. He had fished through the demise of the brook trout into the rise of the brown. And he was well connected with England and the rest of the angling world through his correspondence and readings. So it was natural that he should hear of Frederic M. Halford's crusade for the dry fly in England and his trend-setting books, *Floating Flies and How to Dress Them* (1886), and *Dry Fly Fishing in Theory and Practice* (1889).

A sketch by John Groth based on the only photograph of Theodore Gordon actually in the stream (his home river, the Neversink), depicted coaching his "best chum" in casting to a fish.

Gordon devoured both of Halford's books and wrote to ask him for more information on this new phenomenon. Halford's reply is now fly-fishing history; on February 22, 1890, he sent back a letter offering to help Gordon create new floating patterns specifically for American waters. Clipped to his letter, each identified alongside, were approximately fifty of his favorite dry flies. "And thus," wrote John McDonald, "the dry fly winged its way to the New World."

This event has come to symbolize the arrival of the dry fly in America partly because it involved a dramatic, documentable exchange between two angling giants, but mainly because Gordon used Halford's flies and advice to create the first *American* dry-fly patterns. Actually, Gordon was one of a growing number of Americans who knew of Halford and were

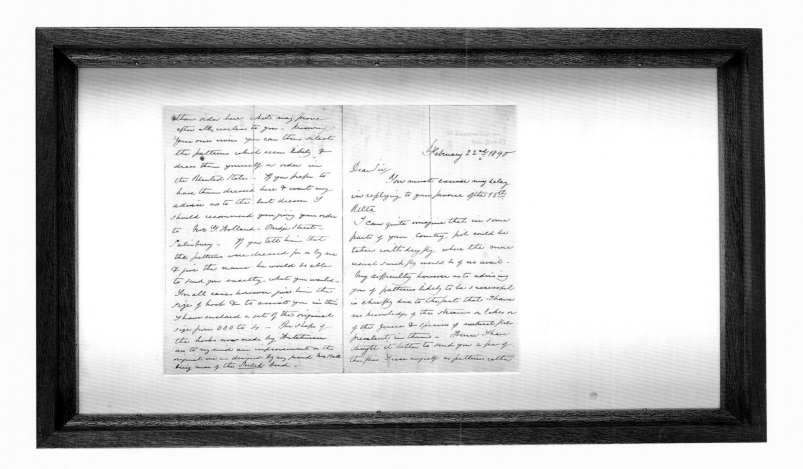

Frederic M. Halford's historic letter sent along with an enclosure of personal favorite dry-fly patterns to Theodore Gordon in 1890. "And thus," wrote John McDonald, "the dry fly winged its way to the New World."

Courtesy Anglers' Club of New York.

experimenting with English dry flies and wets fished dry, beginning with Thad Norris in the early 1860s. Dry-fly articles had already appeared in American periodicals of the 1870s, and the first American books to mention dry-fly tactics and tying were published in the 1880s. What sets Gordon apart from the other early American dry-fly enthusiasts is the fact that *he scrutinized English dry flies and dry-fly tactics and found them unsuited to American trout streams.* So he started from scratch to identify native insects, design new patterns, and perfect his own presentational techniques. Where the others accepted what was available, Gordon was inquisitive, skeptical, and innovative.

When Gordon brought Halford's letter home from the post office, his hands must have trembled as he opened it and viewed the famous dry-fly master's creations—Pale Watery Dun, Little Marryat, Orange Bumble, Jenny Spinner, Welshman's Button, and all the others. "The bacilli or microbe which infects the dry fly entered my system," wrote Gordon, "and the attack which followed was quite severe." He went all-English, with imported rod, dry flies, gossamer silkworm gut, and "all other prescriptions which I presumed necessary to effect a cure," but soon discovered that the English equipment and even the dry-fly tactics were not working to his satisfaction. The insects on which Halford patterned his flies differed from ours, and the placid chalk streams of Hampshire were nothing like the tumbling, freestone streams of the Catskills.

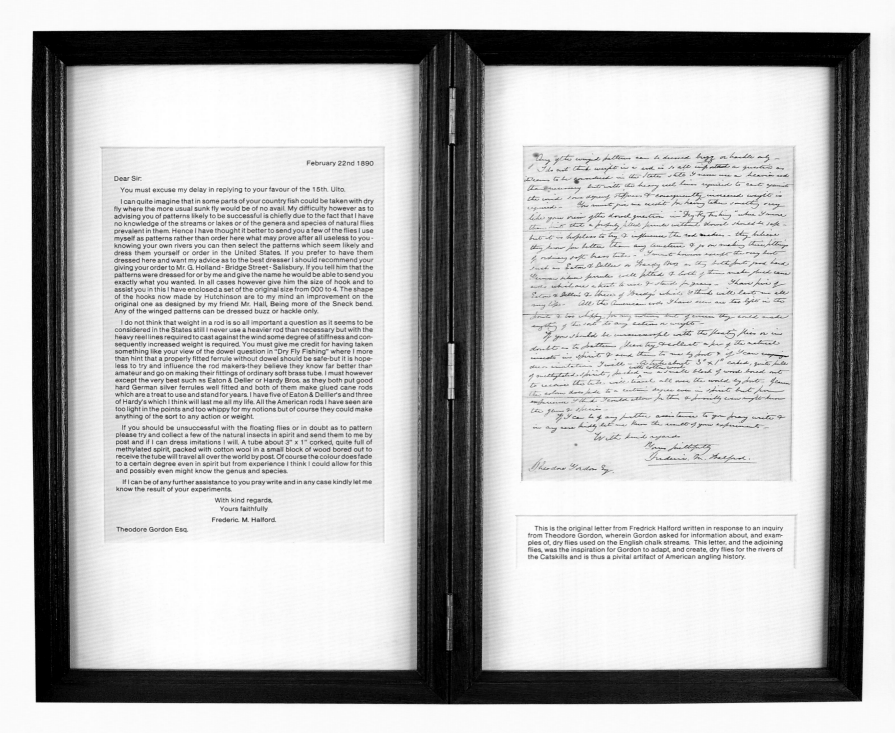

February 22nd 1890

Dear Sir:

You must excuse my delay in replying to your favour of the 15th. Ulto.

I can quite imagine that in some parts of your country fish could be taken with dry fly where the more usual sunk fly would be of no avail. My difficulty however as to advising you of patterns likely to be successful is chiefly due to the fact that I have no knowledge of the streams or lakes or of the genera and species of natural flies prevalent in them. Hence I have thought it better to send you a few of the flies I use myself as patterns rather than order here what may prove after all useless to you - knowing your own rivers you can then select the patterns which seem likely and dress them yourself or order in the United States. If you prefer to have them dressed here and want my advice as to the best dresser I should recommend your giving your order to Mr. G. Holland - Bridge Street - Salisbury. If you tell him that the patterns were dressed for or by me and give the name he would be able to send you exactly what you wanted. In all cases however give him the size of hook and to assist you in this I have enclosed a set of the original size from 000 to 4. The shape of the hooks now made by Hutchinson are to my mind an improvement on the original one as designed by my friend Mr. Hall, Being more of the Sneck bend. Any of the winged patterns can be dressed buzz or hackle only.

I do not think that weight in a rod is so all important a question as it seems to be considered in the States still I never use a heavier rod than necessary but with the heavy reel lines required to cast against the wind some degree of stiffness and consequently increased weight is required. You must give me credit for having taken something like your view of the dowel question in "Dry Fly Fishing" where I more than hint that a properly fitted ferrule without dowel should be safe-but it is hopeless to try and influence the rod makers-they believe they know far better than amateur and go on making their fittings of ordinary soft brass tube. I must however except the very best such as Eaton & Deller or Hardy Bros. as they both put good hard German silver ferrules well fitted and both of them make glued cane rods which are a treat to use and stand for years. I have five of Eaton & Delller's and three of Hardy's which I think will last me all my life. All the American rods I have seen are too light in the points and too whippy for my notions but of course they could make anything of the sort to any action or weight.

If you should be unsuccessful with the floating flies or in doubt as to pattern please try and collect a few of the natural insects in spirit and send them to me by post and if I can dress imitations I will. A tube about 3" x 1" corked, quite full of methylated spirit, packed with cotton wool in a small block of wood bored out to receive the tube will travel all over the world by post. Of course the colour does fade to a certain degree even in spirit but from experience I think I could allow for this and possibly even might know the genus and species.

If I can be of any further assistance to you pray write and in any case kindly let me know the result of your experiments.

With kind regards,
Yours faithfully
Frederic. M. Halford.

Theodore Gordon Esq.

This is the original letter from Fredrick Halford written in response to an inquiry from Theodore Gordon, wherein Gordon asked for information about, and examples of, dry flies used on the English chalk streams. This letter, and the adjoining flies, was the inspiration for Gordon to adapt, and create, dry flies for the rivers of the Catskills and is thus a pivital artifact of American angling history.

Gordon realized that he was now confronted with both a great opportunity and a difficult challenge. Undaunted, he started with the basics, using the English theories as a general guide, and created dry-fly patterns that worked on American streams. For this he had to devise a crude system for classifying stream insects before there was ever an American stream entomology. He bemoaned the lack of such, and the fact that "an angler will often be at a loss in trying to identify an insect which he finds is attractive to the fish." But he persisted in his conviction that "a copy of the natural fly upon the water will often give one a good basket of trout when all other artificial flies are nearly, if not quite, useless."

An incident that occurred on the Beaverkill in 1906 perfectly illustrates this premise. Gordon ran into M.T. Davidson for the first time while both men were fishing. Davidson had raised an exceptionally

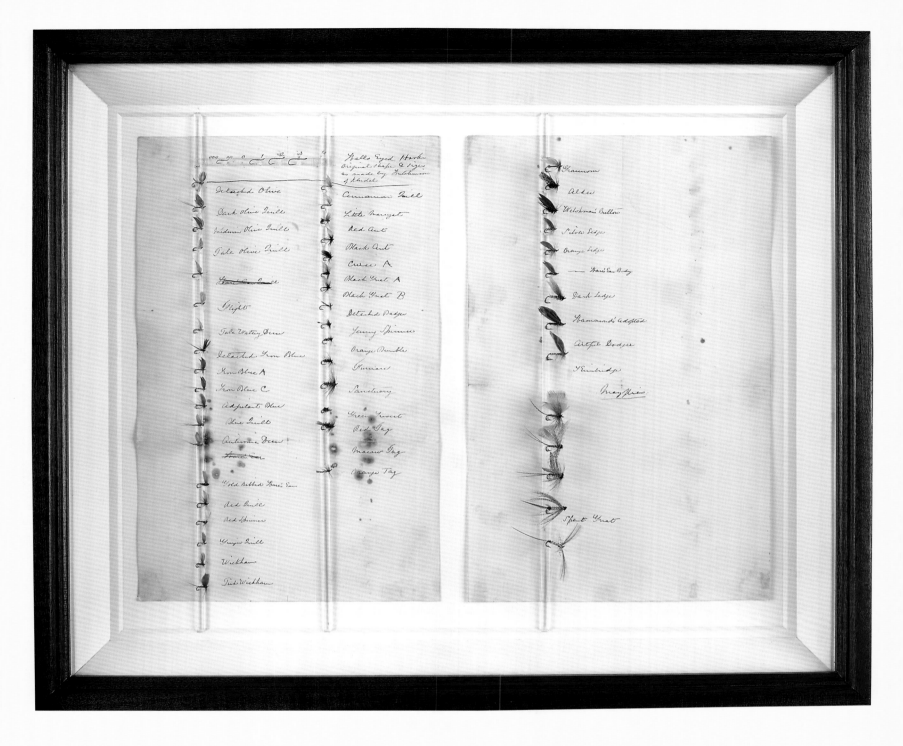

(Left) Page three and a typeset copy of the letter and (above) the approximately fifty dry flies Halford sent to Theodore Gordon in 1890.

Courtesy Anglers' Club of New York.

large fish and, casting repeatedly, had been unable to hook it. He eyed Gordon's tackle, judged that he was a real fisherman, and told him where the big trout was, but Gordon would not fish for it. Instead, he gave a brilliant lesson in matching the hatch, described by Davidson a few years later in a letter to *Forest and Stream*:

> Along the banks grew some willows, and in these Mr. Gordon found several fine specimens of the fly. After securing a large one, Mr. Gordon produced a box of feathers, gut and No. 12 fly hooks. In a remarkably short time he had tied a beautiful duplicate of the original and, handing it to me, insisted that I make another try at the old trout.

Nervously, Davidson tied on Gordon's imitation, cast for, hooked, played, and landed a 20¼-inch, three-pound, eight-ounce trout. The two fishermen went back to Trout Valley Farm, where they ate supper together and where Davidson christened the new fly "Gordon's Fancy," even though "fancy" flies were not supposed to be imitations of real insects.

Creating successful imitations of American stream insects was only half of Gordon's achievement. The other half was working out a dry-fly construction for American streams, where the flies, quoth McDonald, "are always being ducked by white caps, froth, converging currents, and all the movements of the stream." Halford could afford to use softer hackle, for he and his countrymen fished to the rise in quiet water, but Gordon sought a stiffer hackle and tied it as sparsely as the conditions would allow. In so doing, he gave birth to a unique American style of dry-fly tying, later perfected by his Catskill followers into the "Catskill style," typically a No. 12 or No. 14 hook, with a lean body of spun fur or stripped quill, a divided wing of lemon-colored wood-duck flank-feather barbules, and several turns of stiff cock's hackle, usually dun, ginger, or grizzly.

Theodore Gordon's fly box. Soon after Gordon received Englishman Halford's dry flies, he discovered that the insects on which those flies were patterned differed from ours. He thus had to start from scratch, using English theories as a general guide, and create patterns that worked on American streams. Many of the flies in this box are the result.
Courtesy Anglers' Club of New York.

Even though Gordon respected Halford and numbers of other English and American dry-fly experts, he had little patience with the fast-growing "cult of the dry-fly purist." Sometimes he was tolerant: "A few ultra dry fly men may assume airs of superiority, but they are mostly good fellows. I have never known one of them to kill too many trout." Other times, he was not so tolerant, as when he wrote to Halford's wet-fly rival, G.E.M. Skues: "Mr. Halford is like many another. He has become an authority on dry-fly fishing and has been tempted in 'Ethics of the Dry Fly' to speak authoritatively on wet-fly fishing of which he knows nothing. How any man can be such an unmitigated ass as to 'flog' a slow clear river like Test or Itchen downstream, I cannot imagine." Halford had ignored the refinements of wet-fly fishing and characterized the wet-fly man as a "flogger" of the stream, which insulted Gordon's sensibilities.

THEODORE GORDON'S FLY BOX
Presented by William Naden
1955

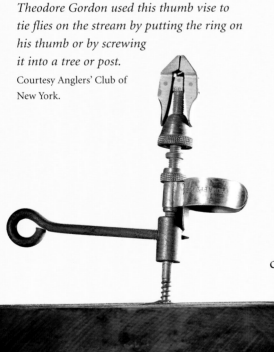

Three months before he died, Gordon wrote to Steenrod, still fretting over the Skues-Halford rivalry:

Mr. Skues did rather a plucky thing some years ago. He worked out a system of wet fly fishing for the chalk dry fly streams, and killed many trout when the dry fly would not work. Then he published a book on "Minor Tactics of the Chalk Streams" that stirred up all the prejudice in the dry fly ranks. Mr. Halford was particularly fierce, and gave Skues (of course not mentioning him) the devil in his last book. I was very sorry as Halford had always been so fair for over 20 years, but he was growing old; for years he had fished only certain preserved lengths of the Test and Itchen. He was recognized as the great authority, and had become a bit prejudiced and dictatorial.

As John McDonald has observed, Theodore Gordon performed in this country the joint services of a Skues and a Halford. He arrived on the scene when Americans were fishing only wet flies and the English were going through a dry-fly revolution. In having brought about the juncture of these two great traditions, Gordon established himself as "the father of modern American angling."

FIFTEEN

Trout Hatcheries

~~~~~~

W e've met "Uncle Thad" Norris, America's best-known nine-teenth-century angler, and Theodore Gordon, the man who redefined American fly fishing. Now meet **Seth Green,** without whom Norris and Gordon would have had little to fish for. Green, quite simply, put the trout back in the streams. In 1837, he discovered how to artificially propagate brook trout, and, in 1864, he built the world's first trout hatchery, still operating today in Caledonia, New York. Green's hatchery was the source of trout to replenish streams that had suffered decades of depreda-tion from logging, tanneries, and the keep-all-you-catch habits of early sport fishers.

Green began in 1835, at the age of eighteen, as a commercial fisherman. He fished the lakes and streams around his home and sold his catch in Rochester. His inventiveness and motivation soon led to the propagation of brook trout in order to meet the demand for more of "the diner's delight." In later years, when he was employed by New York State to raise fish for its lakes and streams, Green became a skilled fly fisherman. Describing his technique, an associate said, "He gazes far off over the rippled water looking after the falling of his fly, as time after time he lifts the long line with a pow-erful yet elegant motion and, winging it far behind him, casts it forward with the perfection of easy force. This is his forte and few may dare to enter the lists against him."

The rearing ponds of the Caledonia hatchery could not have been located in a more conducive environment. Rising out of the limestone strata around Caledonia, the creek bursts full blown out of several springs, some the diameter of a barrel. Its crystal-clear water flows continuously and evenly at temperatures between 43 degrees and 55 degrees all year round. The creek's lime-and-sulfur tincture supports an abundance of

(Above) Fred Mather, superintendent of the Cold Spring Harbor hatchery on Long Island, imported the first brown trout eggs from Europe in 1883 and sent 12,000 to Seth Green, who then stocked the Catskill rivers with their first brown trout.

(Left) Seth Green, "father of American fish culture," discovered artificial propagation of trout and built the world's first trout hatch-ery in Caledonia, New York.

Photographs courtesy A.N. Cheney Collection.

211

watercresses and mosses laden with myriad shrimp, caddis worms, mayfly nymphs, miller's-thumbs, snails, and other trout food.

Green's first "brook shanty" was a crude affair that simply screened off and sheltered a section of the brook as it flowed through a protective enclosure. Then New York State entered the picture in 1868, and the science of fish culture accelerated rapidly. In that year, the state legislators established the New York Fisheries Commission—three years before the U.S. Fish Commission was founded—and Seth Green was appointed one of the three commissioners. His first accomplishment was to persuade the state to appropriate ten thousand dollars for a propagation program to revitalize the streams of New York. The money was used to lease Green's hatchery and to hire him away from his short-lived commissioner's job to become the state's first superintendent of fish culture.

Stone commemorating the 100th anniversary of the Caledonia fish hatchery in 1964. Photograph by the author.

By 1875, the Caledonia facility, now called a "hatching house," had been bought outright by the state and improved with buildings and rearing ponds to such an extent that it was described as "the most economical and largest fish-breeding establishment in the world." Under Seth Green's aggressive management, Caledonia became a widely known center for the exchange of fish and fish-raising techniques.

In 1869, the first international exchange occurred when Caledonia sent a can of brook trout eggs to England. That same year 15 million shad fry were planted by Caledonia in the Hudson River. In 1870, Green survived a roaring gale seventeen miles off the Canadian shore of Lake Ontario, netted thirteen lake trout, stripped them of eighty thousand eggs, and raced back to put them into the Caledonia troughs. When they hatched, he swapped four thousand of the fry with Canada for four thousand Atlantic salmon eggs. A month later he went to Detroit, netted white fish in the St. Clair River, and returned with several boxes of eggs.

In 1871, Seth and his brother Monroe personally accompanied four eight-gallon milk cans of just-hatched shad fry all the way to California. The surviving fry were stocked in the Sacramento River and have multiplied to give the western shad fisherman better fishing than his eastern counterpart. California reciprocated in 1875 with a batch of "mountain trout" (rainbow) eggs, 260 of which lived to become the breeders that supplied not only New York but much of the East. The strain was mingled three years later with 113 so-called McCloud River rainbows that two Caledonia hatcherymen brought back alive from California, having traded 99 mature smallmouth bass, which went into Lake Temescal near Oakland.

The year 1882 typified Seth Green's enterprising nature. Cut off by the state from his annual appropriation, and laden with millions of impregnated California rainbow eggs he could not hatch, Green blanketed the nation with an offer of up to five hundred eggs to "any responsible party for a small packing fee." The response was so great that rainbow eggs were shipped to every state in the country, including California.

In 1883, a year famous in American trouting history, the German brown trout arrived at the Caledonia hatchery via the Cold Spring Harbor hatchery on Long Island. **Fred Mather,** the Cold Spring hatchery manager, shipped twelve thousand of the impregnated eggs he had received from Herr F. von Behr, president of the Deutsche Fisherei Verein in Berlin, to Green in Caledonia. The following year, some of the fingerlings escaped from the Caledonia hatchery, and they are supposed to be the first brown trout ever to be stocked in American waters. The first purposeful stocking of browns in the Catskills was at Aden Brook, a tributary of the Neversink River, in 1886. As we learned earlier, the brown trout along with the dry fly was the salvation of modern American fly fishing.

Seth Green was also an innovator in fish culture. He discovered that the dry process of mixing ova and milt together in a pan without adding water produced a higher yield of fertile eggs and with less effort. He made fixed troughs obsolete by creating "hatching boxes," perforated containers that could be placed at such an angle in flowing water that the resulting

The Caledonia state hatchery today specializes in raising two-year-old brown trout for the public waters of eight New York counties.

Photographs: above by Aerial Views, right by the author.

"rotary ebullition" of the eggs was exactly akin to the motion the eggs received when deposited naturally in a streambed. His most significant innovation was the first cross-breeding of trout in history. Starting in 1877, he failed several times and then, after repeated back-breeding, produced an offspring of the male brook trout and female lake trout that could reproduce itself. Eventually named the "splake," this hybrid combined the larger size of the lake trout with the fighting and table qualities of the brook trout and became a highly popular game fish in the Northeast.

After Seth died in 1888, his brother Monroe carried on as supervisor of the Caledonia hatchery. In true family tradition, he helped establish a shad hatchery in Germany on the Rhine and introduced black bass to English waters for the Duke of Newcastle. However, in spite of the far-flung influence of the Green brothers, their most consistent contribution was made right in their own backyard through the annual stockings of Catskill rivers with "all the salmon tribes of fish." Throughout the years of stream recovery from hemlock deforestation and tannery pollution, Caledonia was the official Catskill hatchery. Testimony to the Green brothers' success is evident in Kit Clarke's 1893 comment: "The Beaverkill and Neversink have yielded more and larger trout than at any time in the past 20 years." Even after 1894, when a hatchery was built on the Beaverkill, Caledonia continued to supply most of the Catskill stocking needs.

How the Beaverkill hatchery site got approved in the first place is something of a mystery. The site selection committee of New York fish commissioners visited several Sullivan County locations in August of 1893. All were in accord that "this section of the State is in the greatest need of a hatchery and liberal planting of trout, as there are endless numbers of splendid trout streams. More summer visitors of the middle classes visit Sullivan County than any other county in the State."

The commissioners came to Roscoe on August 22. They examined Darbee Brook, which runs through the Rockland flats, and found it of insufficient volume. Then one of them asked that they go farther up the flats and test the temperature of the Beaverkill, which had been "spoken of as an elegant trout stream ever since he was a boy."

To the great surprise of the whole party, the water of the Beaverkill registered 59 degrees, while the Willowemoc that same day stood at 71 degrees. "The test being highly satisfactory," according to an eyewitness report, "the Commissioners stayed over night at Rockland, and on the 23rd they located their probable site for the hatchery." Secretary Doyle, who was engineer of the Commissioners, made the remark that they could build a hatchery at Rockland with Beaverkill water, which he thought would be superior in every way to their Caledonia hatchery.

Either political influence or the magic name of the Beaverkill, or

A Trout's Life Begins

In these ingenious photographs, Mark Batur, New York State fisheries biologist, simulated a trout stream in a special aquarium he devised and captured the instant a trout embryo emerges from its "eyed egg" as a "sac fry." Feeding off its little belly-borne food-pouch and—when it is big enough—consuming bugs and other stream foods, the baby trout progresses through the life stages of fingerling and yearling into an adult fish.

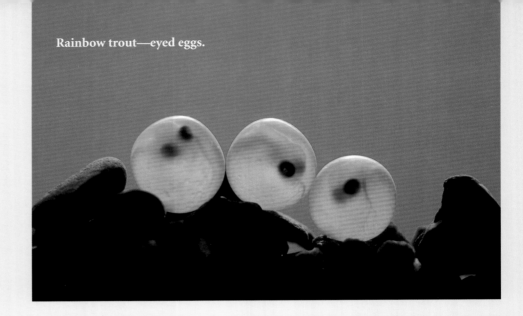

Rainbow trout—eyed eggs.

Rainbow trout—hatching out.

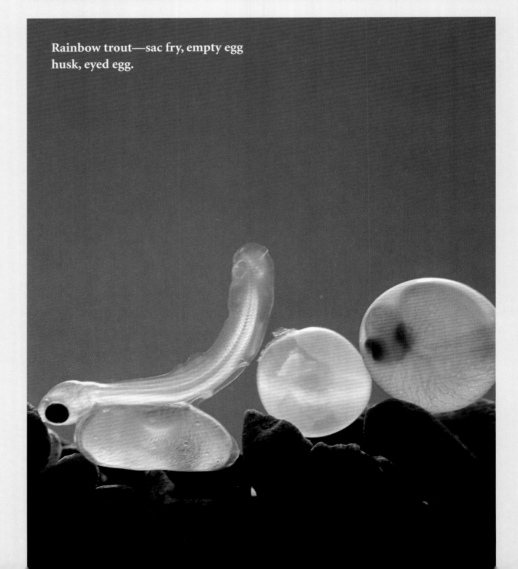

Rainbow trout—sac fry, empty egg husk, eyed egg.

Brown trout—two sac fry in the first seconds of their lives.

Lisa Shaver's hands holding her babies.

This photograph taken at the Beaverkill (Shaver) Trout Hatchery.

(Top) The Beaverkill hatchery that operated at the upper end of the Rockland flats for only nine years and closed due to poor water conditions.
Courtesy New York State Historical Society.

(Bottom) Float stocking enabled the Beaverkill-Willowemoc Rod & Gun Club to distribute fish evenly from Livingston Manor down to East Branch. Harry Darbee, right, holds the boat steady.
Courtesy Judie Darbee Vinciguerra.

both, certainly weighed heavily in this decision, for in 1895, the very first year of operations, the new hatchery started running into problems. It was flooded on April 1 with "one of the worst freshets that had visited that section in twenty-five or thirty years."

In succeeding annual reports, the fish commissioners progressively unfolded the story of a failing hatchery. There were "temperatures above the limit that would sustain trout," inadequate water supply, and general dissatisfaction with productivity, until finally the Beaverkill hatchery was closed in 1904 and a new one built on Whortleberry Creek in Cold Spring Valley (Margaretteville, Delaware County), "a part of the Catskills where there are numerous trout streams, making it an admirable location for distribution."

Following its nine-year abortive effort on the Beaverkill, the state became more conservative in its hatchery location practice. In his 1906 report, the commissioner noted that good hatchery sites were scarce and difficult to find, ending with this revelation: "The difficulty is too often increased by the importunities of persons who have some private interests to advance in the selection of a site, and who bring to bear influences which are entirely foreign to a proper fish cultural policy."

The Delaware hatchery was much more productive than its Beaverkill predecessor. It provided millions of trout for Catskill streams

Seven chapters reveal the special character of each river.

THREE

Beaverkill River

Ten beautiful river maps—also sold separately from the book.

An intimate portrait of the world's first female fly-fishing club.

SEVENTEEN

The Woman Flyfishers Club

Over 250 color photographs of historic Catskill rivers.

Three tackle chapters on classic rods, reels, and flies;

ELEVEN

Reels

Photos, patterns, and origins of 47 classic Catskill flies.

TWELVE

Flies

"Land of Little Rivers will be an instant classic."
Dan Rather, CBS News

Land of Little Rivers

A Story in Photos of Catskill Fly Fishing

AUSTIN McK. FRANCIS

Land of Little Rivers
A Story in Photos of Catskill Fly Fishing

Austin McK. Francis
Enrico Ferorelli, Photographer

A stunning photographic portrait and rich, lucid narrative of the hallowed streams where American fly fishing had its beginnings.

The Beaverkill, Willowemoc, Neversink, Esopus, Schoharie and Delaware—the rivers of angling pioneers Thaddeus Norris, Robert Barnwell Roosevelt, Theodore Gordon, and many others—are celebrated in this gorgeous book of photographs and text. In three major sections, *Land of Little Rivers* presents historical and physical profiles of the rivers; classic rods, reels and flies; and engaging stories of the people, events, and developments that constitute the Catskill fly-fishing tradition.

Francis and Ferorelli have produced an exquisite, museum-quality work, one that captures magnificently the beauty and passion so central to the sport Izaak Walton called "the gentle art."

Book Profile:
280 pages/$100 hardcover/9⅝ x 13 inches/November 1999
265 color photos/55 duotones/29 paintings & drawings/11 color maps
Published by The Beaverkill Press
Printed in Verona, Italy, by Stamperia Valdonega
Distributed to bookstores by W. W. Norton & Co./ISBN 0-393-04855-1

---

well into the 1930s. However, in 1935, during its biological survey of the Delaware and Susquehanna watersheds, the state discovered Toad Basin Spring on Mongaup Creek and decided that it offered even greater potential and a more central location for the Catskill hatchery. The only problem was that Bob Ward, whose brother Charles owned the DeBruce Club Inn, had discovered it earlier and built a private hatchery there. He refused the state's offer to buy him out. When the war came and forced him to shut down, Ward sold, on July 16, 1946, Toad Basin Spring, all the hatchery facilities, and 335 surrounding acres to George H. Treyz, who eventually sold to the state. Over the next few years, the state moved the hatchery closer to the spring source and built what was described at its opening in 1949 as "the most modern fish culture facility in the world." The DeBruce hatchery continues its operations today as the official Catskill trout farm and one of the state's twelve fish hatcheries.

Individuals in the Catskills have played significant roles also in raising trout. Perhaps the most prominent of these was **Edward R. Hewitt.** Instead of pursuing a family tradition of investments and corporate directorships, Hewitt dedicated his inheritance and considerable talent to a lifetime of "making better trout fishing." He bought twenty-seven hundred acres and four miles of the Neversink in 1918 and made it his trout laboratory. For his hatchery he ran a sluiceway from a spring on the hillside into hatching troughs and on into screen-protected rearing and storage ponds. He tapped the same spring and ran it onto the back porch of his fishing camp and through pipe coils he installed in an antique ice box. This was where the day's catch was kept. Mabel Ingalls recalled that he also kept in his ice box the breasts of great blue herons that visited his rearing ponds once too often: "We brought some friends down from Albany one time, and we warned them, 'If he likes you, he'll give you the breast of blue heron, but the trouble is, it's the *blue* breast of blue heron.' It was always really awfully far gone; of course, he had been brought up in the old English grouse tradition where they shoot the grouse and let them hang until they drop off."

In the river, to improve its hospitality to trout, Hewitt built current deflectors, winter holes, and plank dams. His dams were engineering marvels, intricate yet stable, designed to withstand the destructive force

Ed Hewitt working in his trout hatchery on the Neversink. He ran a sluiceway from a spring on the hillside into hatchery troughs and rearing ponds that were screened to keep out predators. Of his Neversink fishery, he said, "I can get more big fish in a week than are taken in the whole Catskill country in a whole season."
Photograph by Henry G. Davis.

of Catskill ice and floods. He built a half dozen or more of them, each creating a large pool of great trout-holding capacity—Dugway, Camp, Molly's, Shop, Flat, Home, and Big Bend. Hewitt stocked these pools with hundreds of big fish—trout of two to six pounds—and at the end of the season it was his custom to catch out as many as he could and winter them in his rearing ponds, safe from the destructive Neversink floods. Said Sparse Grey Hackle, "We whom he used to invite to help him used heavy rods, strong leaders, and bait; and we horsed our fish out and into carrying cans as quickly as possible so as not to exhaust them with long play."

Hewitt's Neversink experiments in raising fish produced many useful findings, often stated with his characteristic assuredness:

Natural raising conditions. "I do not believe we can grow hatchery fish which will make good long-lived stream fish unless we give them plenty of room in the water and feed them largely on their own natural diets."

Attracting insects. "A small electric light hung low over the water will attract vast numbers of insects and be surrounded by slashing fish all night. This is a very easy and cheap way of feeding trout."

What makes a trout. "Few fishermen realize that it takes four or five pounds of insects to make one pound of trout. Trout are fat fish. Where bass and perch are only 1 or 2 percent fat, the normal trout is 10 to 11 percent fat."

Vermin. "A constant war has to be waged against them. A kingfisher will consume two or three thousand fry in a season. They are very easily gotten rid of by putting one or two posts in shallow water in the pond

The Catskill state fish hatchery on Mongaup Creek.

Aerial photographs below and right enabled by Roger Lynker.

and setting a steel trap on top. They light on these traps and are readily caught. I asked my man what he had caught while I was away one year. He reported seventeen kingfishers, three owls, three herons, and one crane."

Cocksure though he was, Hewitt contributed much to hatchery science and more broadly to fisheries management. He was among the first to advise limiting one's kill as a way of "making better trout fishing." He had a singularly effective way of making sure that not too many of his own fish got taken out of the Neversink. He usually kept a close eye on his guests and when a good-sized fish was reeled in, he waded right out and released it, with the chagrined angler gaping in silent protest.

There is still a Beaverkill Hatchery, though far different from its unfortunate 1890s namesake. Started by **Fred Shaver** in 1962, the present-day Beaverkill Hatchery is situated on Alder Creek, a tributary of the upper Beaverkill River. Now being operated by the third and fourth generations of Shavers, the hatchery has grown into one of the largest privately owned trout hatcheries in New York State. Beaverkill Hatchery supplies browns, brooks, rainbows, goldens, and tiger trout to fly-fishing clubs, municipalities, and restaurants throughout the Northeast. It hatches some 350,000 trout eggs each year of all its varieties, of which approximately two-thirds survive to please many thousands of both diners and anglers who seek the joys of trout.

The Beaverkill Trout Hatchery sign is painted on the blade from a long-gone Turnwood, New York, sawmill, where the hatchery (below) has been run since 1962 by four generations of Shavers.
Courtesy the Shaver family.

Kayla . . . the world's only trout-herding dog.

At Beaverkill Trout Hatchery, Lisa Shaver's eleven-year-old Labrador, Kayla, while watching Lisa herd trout into a holding net, taught herself to do the same. Once the fish are in the net, Lisa measures and grades them for restaurant and fishing-club customers. Those that don't make the grade get thrown back to Kayla, who gently clamps each fish in her soft jaws and thrusts it back into the pond. Kayla has never injured a single trout. More amazingly, Kayla is now teaching Maggie, a two-year-old yellow Lab, the tricks of trout herding.

(Top to bottom) Herding and corralling . . .

(Left to right) Grading and returning . . .

(Left to right) Kayla dunks them back . . .

Good dog!

Containing 125 years of fishing memories, this is the sitting room of Salmo Fontinalis, formed in 1873 as the first of the Beaverkill stream clubs.
Courtesy Salmo Fontinalis.

SIXTEEN
Private Clubs & Preserves

Three main forces were at work in the emergence of private fishing clubs and family preserves in the Catskills. In the early 1870s, two railroads were completed on either side of the headwaters of the Rondout, Neversink, Esopus, Willowemoc, and Beaverkill rivers, opening up many miles of the region's choicest concentration of trout waters to "rodsters" from the city.

Also, the Catskill economic base was slowly but permanently changing. From the era of the old river industries that saw the rise of tanneries, rafting, and wood-acid factories, the Catskill economy had always depended largely on distant consumers. Moreover, when industrialization and modern technology put an end to these livelihoods and to many of the farms, the same forces created a leisure class that supplied new consumers in the form of weekenders, vacationers, and sportsmen. However, for the native Catskiller, this was a period of hardship and uncertainty.

Many thousands of acres owned by the tanning, lumbering, and wood-acid operators were abandoned after the trees were gone and the industries displaced by more modern processes. When taxes on these properties remained unpaid long enough, the lands came up at tax sales. Small farms also became available, such as those that had grown hay to feed loggers' oxen, and those tucked away in narrow, cul-de-sac valleys of the sort that give rise to trout streams.

Absentee owners began appearing on the Catskill tax maps, where formerly the landowners had been almost entirely local residents. In fact, the Catskill Forest Preserve, owned by New York State, got its start in 1885 when no one would buy a huge chunk of abandoned acreage in Ulster County.

225

Furlough Lake (left and above), nestled in Dry Brook valley, attracted George J. Gould, son of railroad magnate Jay Gould, to put together in the 1880s a three-thousand-acre estate and fishing preserve.

(Right) Furlough Lodge, the twenty-six-room lodge built by George Gould in 1890, is now the home of his grandson and wife, Mary and Kingdon Gould, Jr.

Photographs courtesy the Gould family.

The log cabin built in 1889 by Ben Hardenburgh, supposedly as a love nest for a wealthy New Yorker, whom Ben threw out upon learning its intended use; he then leased it to a group of Brooklyn fishermen who made it the headquarters for their new club.

Courtesy Fly Fishers Club of Brooklyn.

With increasing competition for elbow room on the trout streams, it was natural that many of these new owners should be wealthy New York fishermen establishing their own mountain retreats and private trout preserves. They were further stimulated by the growing recognition that fly fishing was a sport for gentlemen and was enjoyed by members of England's nobility, so admired by socially climbing Americans.

Anthony W. Dimock, author of *Wall Street and the Wilds*, located his haven at Peekamoose on upper Rondout Creek, one valley over from the Neversink. In the introduction to his book, he created a vivid picture of the conflicting forces in a city-based angler's life:

> *It was the dream of my life to live in the wilds and even during my greatest activity in business I was looking forward to a time when my taste could be gratified. The opportunity came in the seventies, for while on a fishing trip I found a valley in the Catskills so surrounded by mountains and shut in by trees that it promised all the seclusion I could ask. From the nearest railroad station but ten miles of mountain road remained, and as I traveled it my troubles fell away.*
>
> *I ran a telegraph wire through the woods from the nearest station and the sounder in my room was a comfort when it didn't sound. My*

family was happy in their sylvan surroundings but they came to hate that sounder, for they learned its language and knew when it called me to the city in tones not to be disregarded.

On one such occasion I started in the blackness of a rainy night for a ten mile tramp over a dangerous road to the little village of Shokan. It was near midnight when I arrived, the town was asleep, and I had to arouse several people before I could find one who would drive me to Rondout, eighteen miles away. At that place I hired a negro to commandeer a boat, in the owner's absence, and row me across the Hudson to Wheatsheaf, where I hired another man to take me to Poughkeepsie, reaching that town in time to take the owl train for New York.

One of the larger and more elaborate Catskill hunting and fishing preserves was that of George J. Gould, son of railroad magnate Jay Gould, located at Furlough Lake on Dry Brook, a headwater stream of the East Branch of the Delaware. In 1890, when he was still in his twenties, Gould bought 550 acres, and within several years he had expanded his holding to over 3,000 acres. Centered on the 30-acre lake, he built a 26-room, 2½-story, log-and-stone house, log stable, and boathouse. There was also an enclosed "deer park" stocked with Colorado elk and Virginia and black-tailed deer, outside which roamed the native white-tailed deer. One of the sights most intriguing to his visitors, according to a *New York Times* reporter who had just toured the newly opened lodge, was "a dovecote with 2,000 doves and pigeons of every sort and kind, harmoniously living together in a many-storied, handsome building that looks like a first-class New York apartment house."

Founding members of the Fly Fishers Club of Brooklyn gathered on their porch around 1900. From the left: James Rice, Jr., H.B. Marshall, Richard "Pop" Robbins, B.J. Scholerman, E.J. Allen, Frank Perkins, and a guest, George M.L. LaBranche.
Courtesy Fly Fishers Club of Brooklyn.

Over on the Neversink, numerous small farms were bought and combined into the "country seats" of well-to-do city sportsmen. The larger preserves, of several thousand acres each, were established by Clarence Roof in 1882 on the West Branch and by Raphael Govin in 1898 on the East Branch.

On the Willowemoc, there was the Ward estate at DeBruce, and the Van Norden property farther up on the headwaters at Lake Willowemoc (now Sand Pond). The Van Nordens and their relatives the Van Brunts started the Willowemoc Club, which also owned, over in the Beaverkill valley, Balsam Lake, Thomas Pond (now Beecher Lake), and several miles of the stream. The club members used to walk back and forth across the three miles of mountaintop separating the two rivers and their lakes.

In addition to the single-owner estates, groups of wealthy anglers began forming clubs in the Catskills shortly after the railroads opened up the region. These were "club corporations," established under New York State law, with the right to issue stock, contract debt, limit liability, and, in particular, to own river mileage and fishing rights. In a larger context, fishing clubs were patterned on the many other social clubs being formed mainly by urban businessmen in the late 1800s. There were city, suburban, and rural clubs for dining, athletics, golf, polo, yachting, shooting, hunting, and fishing. An article in the *New York Sun* on May 18, 1890, called attention to this trend as "a modern novelty" and stated that an average of ten groups a day were filing papers for incorporation as clubs with the secretary of state's office in Albany.

"A large fireplace occupies a third of the room's width, with a heavy arch springing from the floor on either side. In the huge recess . . . are two iron dogs upon which rest large, blazing logs."—From a 1900 newspaper article.

Courtesy Fly Fishers Club of Brooklyn.

Salmo Fontinalis was the first of the Beaverkill stream clubs. It was formed in 1873 on the upper river. In 1883, it was joined upstream by the Balsam Lake Club, whose founding members included the Van Nordens and Van Brunts of Willowemoc Lake. The Fly Fishers Club of Brooklyn was incorporated in 1895 by a group of Brooklyn fishermen and moved into Ben Hardenburgh's log cabin on the Beaverkill above Roscoe. An article in the March 20, 1904, edition of the *Brooklyn Daily Eagle* included this notice: "James Rice, Jr., a founder of the Brooklyn Fly Fishers, was for years a very successful bait fisher at Henryville. When he discovered this famous section of the Beaverkill and the club was organized, he swore off bait and has ever since been a fly caster of great skill." Chancellor Levison and Charles Bryan, both charter members of the Brooklyn group, and several of their club mates, are credited with instrumental roles in the 1906 founding of the Anglers' Club of New York.

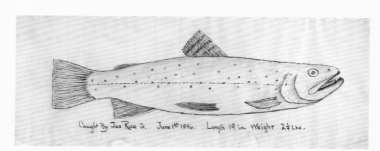

James Rice memorialized his trout with this primitive drawing and started his club's tradition of sketching and displaying their big trout.

Courtesy Fly Fishers Club of Brooklyn.

Caught By Jas Rice Jr. June 1st 1896: Length 19 in Weight 2¾ Lbs.

In 1875, the Beaverkill (Fishing) Association was organized at farmer Voorhess's homestead just below Lew Beach. In 1910, one of its members

"Sitting on the porch" has a special meaning for club members, who relax here after coming off the stream.
Courtesy Fly Fishers Club of Brooklyn.

bought out Voorhess, and the group eventually became the Beaverkill Trout Club. And, in 1959, Clear Lake Club was formed out of the old Marble estate on the river opposite the lake of the same name.

On Mill Brook, a tributary of the East Branch of the Delaware, a group of New York businessmen formed the Tuscarora Club in 1901 by purchasing a bankrupt farm, boardinghouse, and sawmill. At the source of Esopus Creek, several Kingston and Albany sportsmen founded Winnisook Lodge in the late 1800s. On the Neversink, Ed Hewitt converted his river property into the Big Bend Club in 1947. And, on Willowemoc Creek in 1936, having incorporated as the Woman Flyfishers Club four years earlier, a group of pioneering female anglers set up their first headquarters, later moving briefly to the Rondout before settling down on the West Branch of the Neversink. Farther down on the Willowemoc, a group of fishing friends who frequented Ward's DeBruce Club Inn organized the DeBruce Fly Fishing Club in 1959 when the inn went out of business.

(Top left) The DeBruce Fly Fishing Club seen across one of its ponds. This club was formed by regulars of Ward's DeBruce Club Inn who bought Ward's water and property in the late 1950s and set up their clubhouse in one of the inn's guest cabins.
Courtesy DeBruce Fly Fishing Club.

(Bottom left) Clear Lake Club (1959), originally the Iroquois Club, located on the old Marble estate on the Beaverkill opposite its eponymous lake.
Courtesy Clear Lake Club.

(Above) Beaverkill Trout Club, which grew out of the Beaverkill (Fishing) Association, was formerly the Voorhess family farm located on the Gee and Voorhess brooks downriver from Lew Beach.
Courtesy Beaverkill Trout Club.

Catskill fishing clubs range in size from seven to sixty-three members; in later years membership roles have tended to increase in order to support rising taxes and upkeep. Stream mileage owned or leased by the clubs ranges from about a mile to seven miles. Women guests, anglers or otherwise, are welcome in varying degrees; some of the clubs are set up to accommodate couples and families; however, a few are very tenacious about their long tradition as fraternal retreats.

The first Catskill fishing clubs were more social than sporting, combining the virtues of a wilderness camp, a quiet pond, and gentlemanly recreation. Indeed, three of the four earliest clubs were situated on small lakes, up away from the stream.

At Samuel Coykendall's Alder Lake estate, for example, a festive gathering was recalled by Joshua Gerow in his book *Alder Lake*:

After dinner, when the evening air became cool and wisps of gossamery fog hovered lightly over the placid surface of the lake, emulating the Great Blue Heron that glided over a few hours before, the Coykendalls and their guests strolled down the lantern lighted winding path to the

"Balsam Lake was oval-shaped, scarcely more than half a mile long and a quarter of a mile wide, but presented a charming picture, with a group of dark gray hemlocks filling the valley about its head, and the mountains rising above and beyond."
—JOHN BURROUGHS
Courtesy Balsam Lake Club.

(Above) Balsam Lake Club (1883) is situated at the river's headwaters and was reached in its early days by a rough wagon road over the mountain from Seager in Dry Brook valley.
Courtesy Balsam Lake Club.

Cornelius Van Brunt, founding member and first president of the Balsam Lake Club, standing on his club-house porch.
Courtesy Balsam Lake Club.

boathouse. Here in the spacious, cypress-paneled dance room, decorated with a profusion of multi-colored Japanese lanterns overhanging the water of the lake, the soiree or ball was held. The latest dances, including the cake-walk, turkey-trot, waltz, two-step and, of course, the masquerade, were enjoyed till the oil burned low in the lamps that lighted the room and the path to the Lodge.

Theodore Gordon was unknown to the likes of Coykendall and members of the gentlemen's clubs; for them the art of angling had not yet begun its technical revolution. Recalling the early members of his club, who fished in the late 1800s, one Balsam Lake member wrote:

> Few, if any, professed to be skillful fishermen. They loved the woods, the birds, the beauty of the place, and as they could catch all the small fish they wanted, but no large ones no matter how they tried, no one studied the angler's art. They were men of affairs, exceptionally well read, and enjoyed the company as well as the fishing.

Outsiders, especially those who might once have fished the water now preserved by the clubs, viewed these gentlemen in a different light. One of them said: "You can generally tell the health of the stock market by the number of fancy-pants fishermen along the Beaverkill; they vary in direct proportion to the Dow Jones averages." Others were not so kind:

The ponds and buildings of Wintoon, a four-thousand-acre preserve with five miles of trout stream assembled by Clarence Roof in the 1880s from small farms in the valley of the West Branch of the Neversink.
Courtesy the Frank Connell family.

Not many of them were fishermen but were leaders, tycoons of business, and political bigwigs who devoted most of their time at the Lodge with Old Crow and Canadian Club and were seen strutting about the lawn in their Prince Alberts and derby hats, twirling their canes or twisting their moustaches as suited their vanity, not knowing that in nature a pauper is as good as a prince.

All these clubs are still in existence. Others that were formed and did not survive include: on the Beaverkill, Quill Gordon Associates, Whirling Dun Camp, Beaver Meadow Fly Fishing Club, Colchester Fisheries Club, Saugerties Club, Beaverkill Flyfishers, Beaverkill Trout and Skeet Club; on the Willowemoc, the Willowemoc Club; on the Esopus, Jocelyn Country Club ("an active angling club"); on the Rondout, the Peekamoose Fishing Club, which was started in 1880 and disbanded fifteen years later; and on the East Branch of the Neversink, of the same vintage, the Hamilton Club, which was described in the

Wintoon's main lodge; John Burroughs visited here when Frank Connell was in her early teens, telling her, "I know of no mountain retreat so enticing as Wintoon as long as you are its presiding spirit."
Courtesy the Frank Connell family.

Clarence Roof with his sporting equipment. A New York olive oil importer, Roof lived in Lakewood, New Jersey, in the winter and came to the Neversink because he liked the wild country, especially horseback riding.
Courtesy the Frank Connell family.

(Above) Winnisook Lake looking south down the Big Indian valley from the porch of the main lodge. In 1896, the lake was stocked with one thousand brook trout caught for one cent each out of the Neversink by two members' young sons.

(Left) Winnisook Lake, nestled between Hemlock and Shacklemoose mountains at the head of Esopus Creek, is home to some twenty cabins of members of the Winnisook Club, started in 1886.

(Right) The "New House," built by Winnisook member Tom Evans, festooned by club members at its christening in 1896.

All photographs courtesy the Winnisook Club and Herb Shultz.

Sand Pond, formerly Willowemoc Lake, setting of the earliest private fishing club in the Catskills, the Willowemoc Club, formed in 1870. The double-log-walled cabin built by Warner Van Norden in 1935 lies at the fourteen-acre lake's head.

1890s as "going to seed and the tender mercies of the porcupines."

That so many clubs have survived the varied threats to their continuity is testimony to the durability of the institution. The appeal most often cited by fishing-club members is the congeniality of their club mates, followed closely by the serenity and beauty of their surroundings. Fly fishing and trout are taken for granted; these exist with or without the club privilege.

In the opinion of a private-club member, one I know to be eminently fair minded, "the fact that there has been a balance of private ownership is a large part of what has kept the quality of the Catskills."

In the long run, whatever their justification, these private enclaves have played the role of steward. They have helped preserve the pristinity of these wilderness rivers and protect them as spawning grounds for wild trout, and they have acted as guardians of one of the world's most revered angling traditions.

(Right) The forlorn Alder Lake house built around 1900 by financier and railroad owner Samuel D. Coykendall, who, "inspired by his Dutch ancestors, went into the 'kaatskills' to love, play and perhaps occasionally, to 'tip the wicked flagon.'"

(Below) Alder Lake, seen from next to the Coykendall mansion, a pristine wilderness setting owned today by New York State.
Photograph by the author.

SEVENTEEN

The Woman Flyfishers Club

~~~~~~~~~~~~~~~~~~~~~~~~~~~~~~~~~~~~~

Jane Smith was sitting in the Icelandic Airlines lounge at the Reykjavík airport waiting for her husband and their flight back to New York. It was the summer of 1975, and they had been fishing salmon on the Leirasveit. Another fisherman came along and, noticing her rod case, engaged in the usual where-and-what-luck conversation. He further noticed that she was wearing a gold pin with a fly on it.

"What kind of a fly is that?" he asked.

"A Rat-Faced McDougall," she answered.

"Is that a club emblem?"

"Yes, the Woman Flyfishers Club."

"What is this club anyway, a woman's lib organization?"

Mrs. Smith pulled herself erect in her seat and, in measured tones, replied, "We are a club incorporated in 1932. Our members are all dedicated women fly fishers. We have our own clubhouse and water and we fish all over the world."

The Woman Flyfishers Club was conceived by Julia Freeman Fairchild, Frank Hovey-Roof Connell, and Mary Ashley Hewitt as a way of extending the enjoyment they got from fishing with their husbands, two of whom were members of the Anglers' Club of New York. As recalled by Mrs. Fairchild, one day in 1931 they were seated on the porch at "Wintoon," the fishing preserve assembled by Clarence Roof in the early 1880s on the West Branch of the Neversink. "We started talking about how much fun the men had in their club," said Mrs. Fairchild, "and we said, 'Let's form a club of our own!' So, a small group of us got together at the Hewitts' downstream on the main Neversink and made up a list of women we knew who enjoyed fishing. Later that year we had the details worked out and on January 28, 1932, we were officially incorporated with thirty-three founding members."

The Woman Flyfishers Club, with Julia Fairchild as its first president, was an instant success. The following year they raised their dues and

The Woman Flyfishers' clubhouse on the West Branch of the Neversink, described by one of its members as "a sweet place, the neatest little two-story affair with every comfort and the crispiest curtains and fluffiest blankets."

Courtesy The Woman Flyfishers Club.

took in twenty-two more members. Quite a few of the members had
husbands or fathers who fished and who owned private water or
belonged to fishing clubs; so even though they had no headquarters of
their own at first, they received invitations right away to fish many of the
choicest streams of the Northeast. Ironically, the husbands rarely got to
fish each other's water, which led one of them, Dr. Whittington Gorham,
to nickname his wife and her club mates "The Lady Wanglers."

Mrs. Fairchild and her directors had been searching from the outset
for a "home pool" for their fellow members, and in 1936 they found it
on the upper Willowemoc, above its junction with Fir Brook. As she
remembered it:

> The property belonged to Mrs. Walter Bolling of Alabama and was
> about to be sold for taxes. She was very ill at the time and the negotia-
> tions were tedious and prolonged, but we finally got possession. Along
> with the lease we inherited a caretaker who could talk more and do less
> than anyone I ever knew.

The Bolling place contained 265 acres and one mile of stream. Three
more miles of private water were made available through the courtesy
of the Willowemoc Fishing Club. By 1937 the women had hired a new
caretaker, fixed up the house, stocked the stream, and they were in business. Until 1946, the Willowemoc was the home of the Woman Flyfishers

Club. Then Mrs. Bolling came back, terminated their lease, and reclaimed her house. Said Mrs. Fairchild, "We had a lot of fun there and left it with regret, especially as we had no home to go to and the future looked dim."

To the rescue came Ed Hewitt, who had a soft spot for women anglers. He had heard of some water in the valley next to the Neversink and quickly arranged a merger for the homeless anglers with new landlords in a "little red house" on Sundown Creek, a tributary of the Rondout. Unfortunately, the fishing turned out to be disappointing, especially as the stream had not been posted until the Flyfishers took over, and they would often arrive "just in time to see a poacher sneaking away with a heavy string of trout trailing a large hook festooned with worms."

Discomfort on the Sundown led to restlessness, to continued searching, and finally to the West Branch of the Neversink, less than two miles upstream from where the club was born. In 1950, Frank Connell graciously offered the upper end of her Neversink water complete with clubhouse to her fellow members, and the women anglers came home to their native stream. They are there still, over eighty members strong, having recently observed their sixty-seventh anniversary.

A member of the Woman Flyfishers Club excites a great deal of curiosity when it is revealed that she belongs to the first-ever organization of female fly fishers in the world. She is often asked, for example, how

The Woman Flyfishers Club gathered for their 1955 Outing at the Campfire Club. Kneeling: Talia Manser, Connie Terry, Martha Bulkley, Ann Ordway. Standing: Julia Fairchild, Vega Juhring, Jane Smith, Gladys Straus, Betty Jennings, Margaret Walbridge, Martha Averett, Mary Geyer, Candace Stevenson.

Courtesy The Woman Flyfishers Club.

she got started fishing. It used to be that a female fly fisher took up the sport because she grew up in a sporting family, or was drawn into it by romance. "What started me fishing?" pondered a woman angler. "Love wielding a fly rod; four years later I cast well enough to marry."

Mabel Ingalls, a granddaughter of J.P. Morgan and member of the Flyfishers, did her first fishing around 1915 at summer camp in the Adirondacks. She remembered catching two small fish, on dropper flies, on a backcast. "I really started fishing seriously through boyfriends," she said. "Only 'boyfriend' didn't mean the same thing then as it does today. These were just nice boys who were friends; sex was not involved, certainly not. But all kinds of fun things were—like camping, hunting, and fishing.

"We fished with a group of young men who had gotten out of Harvard, been in the war, and were back in New York in business. Two of them would ask two of us, or maybe there would be three boys and three girls. We took the West Shore Railroad at noon on Saturday, because they all had to work Saturday mornings, and we got off some place near Bear Mountain, fishing various places the boys had been going to alone. They knew the streams."

Reflecting on their outings and relationships with male anglers, Julia Fairchild said, "I think there is an equality of sexes in fishing that is entirely different from any other sport. We never had the slightest feeling with any of our fishing men that we weren't just as good as they were. In fact, it never occurred to any of us that we were men or women; we were fishermen."

In spite of this equality there are certain personality traits commonly associated with men and outdoor sports that a woman must possess if she hopes to be a successful angler. She must be self-reliant. "One of the things Julia was very firm on," said Jane Smith, "was that we were women who were not dependent on anybody but ourselves. We were expected to take care of our own equipment, to know what flies we had, to clean our own fish in places where they didn't have somebody to do it for us. This made quite an impression on me; we didn't come up and forget our wading sneakers."

A Flyfisher is also expected to cope with the physical stress and dis-comforts of an outdoor sport. She should have an appetite for hiking, wading, and long sessions of casting. She knows how to have fun in spite of rainstorms, biting insects, cuts, and bruises. In short, she is a good sport, a rugged individual.

If women anglers are so little different from men anglers, and so at ease in their company, why should there be any reason for them to start their own club? What is the rationale for a women-only fishing club? "I think it is the same for women as for men," said Jane Smith. "There is a certain kind of fellowship that seems to be present if there is only one sex. Once you get rid of the men, there's a kind of letting down of effort to appear anything but what you are."

Angling by its nature is a sport for escapists. "It's my secret life," said Tappen Fairchild, and he introduced his wife, Julia, to a world of privacy and solitude. She and her fishing friends embraced this world and intensified its pleasures by forming their own club. In it, they enjoy the freedom to be themselves, to abandon care, and to recapture the joy and innocence of their youth.

Bookplate designed in 1939 for her club mates by Marguerite Kirmse Cole.
Courtesy The Woman Flyfishers Club.

*Jim Deren fishing Mountain Pool
on the lower Beaverkill, 1955.*
Photograph by Ed Pfizenmaier.

EIGHTEEN

A Cast of Anglers

In spite of **Theodore Gordon's** talents as a flytier and reporter, he shunned attention for both and focused them rather on enhancing his fishing pleasure. His musings revealed a private, lonely man who had few fishing companions:

> It is rather annoying to have spectators overlooking our sport. We prefer to be alone with nature, with perhaps one good friend somewhere in the same stream. It is pleasant to have a chum to lunch with and to share the homeward tramp. Then perhaps we realize for the first time that we are weary and the miles are not so long if we can chat and rehearse the striking events of the day.

Other than Gordon's female fishing "chum," with whom his only fishing photographs were taken, he had three Catskill fishing companions. About Bruce Leroy, one of them, all we know is that he inherited a farm in the Neversink valley but preferred hunting and fishing to farming. The other two were Roy Steenrod and Herman Christian.

Roy Steenrod went to work in the Liberty post office in 1904 and met Gordon by having to handle his mail ("ten to twelve letters a day") and through selling him foreign money orders with which to buy English fly-tying materials. Gordon taught only one person ever how to tie flies, and that was Steenrod, making him swear "on his honor not to tell anybody" the hints and tips he had been given. On his afternoons off from the post office, Steenrod used to walk the five miles from Liberty to Bradley and spend the afternoons with Gordon.

For **Herman Christian,** fishing was an integral part of living, along with hunting, trapping, and subsistence farming. He was born on the Rondout and reared on the Neversink, and he lived to be one of the all-time greats among Catskill fishermen. Christian fished regularly with Gordon, often showing him the lies of big fish. Gordon had great respect for his friend's fishing abilities. In a letter to Roy Steenrod, he wrote: "Christian is a great expert, and has more patience and perseverance

than any other man I ever met. This is the secret of his big fish. That and
going for them *at the correct time.* I think he deserves the big trout he
catches and am glad to see them when he brings them to me to show."

Whenever Christian located "a nice big fish," he took Gordon there
the next day to fish for it. On one occasion, Christian saw "a couple of
good trout in a hole about a mile below Neversink."

*I took Mr. Gordon down there and he got one fish, a 16-inch fish, and
I think I got the other one later, in the middle of June, at night on a
No. 6 dun fly. It was 29½ inches long and weighed 8 pounds 4 ounces.*

George M. L. LaBranche was every bit as dedicated a fisherman as
Theodore Gordon, but he had a different philosophy about fame. He
sought it and won it for his abilities and theories as a dry-fly angler. His
achievements and his authorship of *The Dry Fly and Fast Water* established him as the country's leading expert on dry-fly techniques. It all
began in 1899 when he cast his first dry fly at the mouth of Mongaup
Creek, a tributary of Willowemoc Creek, more as a reaction to the
immediate fishing situation "than to any predevised plan for attempting
the feat."

His feat and the resulting book were to catapult LaBranche into
the forefront of American dry-fly practitioners. As Sparse Grey Hackle
observed, "George, more than any other man, revolutionized the great
American sport of fishing with the fly, for he was the creator and
prophet of what is still the distinctive and unique American school
of dry-fly angling."

LaBranche earned his fame with several developments in angling
technique adapted to America's faster, more turbulent streams. He
shifted the emphasis from the physical aspects of the artificial fly to

the manner of its presentation—its exact placement on the current, which is the fish's food lane. He cast his flies to the places where fish should lie rather than waiting for a fish to begin rising to natural flies, as preferred on the chalk streams of England. And he popularized the "artificial hatch," making cast after cast until a trout could no longer resist the procession of his flies.

Harry Darbee, on the other hand, was more like Herman Christian in that he fished instinctively, and by doing so he often made unaided

discoveries. For example, there was the day he was fishing on the East Branch of the Delaware before it had been dammed. He had fished most of the day with no success, in fact not having even seen a fish. Then, as he left the river, he noticed that the tall grass and willows were loaded with newly emerged stoneflies. The nymphs had crawled ashore to hatch without the fish having started to feed on them. So, the following morning, Harry went down to the same stretch at daybreak. As he told it, "I didn't have a good stonefly pattern, so I took an Edson Dark Tiger bucktail, clipped the hair off even with the hook bend, and pulled the tail out. The brown and yellow result must have looked good, because the two trout, one 17½ inches and one 21 inches, that I caught in less than an hour, were gorged with stonefly nymphs."

Jim Deren was instinctive too. For him, an "angler at heart" was the best thing you could be. When Ian Frazier asked him what distinguishes an angler at heart from the 54 million other people who then fished in the country, Deren said, "It's the call of the wild, the instinct of the hunt. It's a throwback to

June 1, 1978: Lee Wulff having his fish measured by John Adams in a neighborhood fishing competition on the upper Beaverkill.

the forest primeval. It's the feeling of being in a state of grace in a magnificent outdoor cathedral. Either you have it or you don't—it's inborn. The first time I went into the woods, it was as if I had been there before. I could sit all day and watch a field mouse fifteen feet away, watch a bird in a tree huntin' bugs—sometimes they're comical as hell. The woods are a constant unfolding story. The romance of fishing isn't all just fish."

Ed Zern, emerging from the upper Beaverkill. For over thirty years, Zern wrote the "Exit Laughing" column for Field & Stream. *Accused one time of not always being truthful in his column, Zern replied, "I get all the truth I need in the newspaper every morning, and every chance I get I go fishing, or swap stories with fishermen, to get the taste of it out of my mouth."*
Photograph by Sandra Weiner.

Delaware angling friends: Ross Francis, the author, Frank McEneaney, Pam and Will Waller.
Photograph by Page Waller.

NINETEEN

Dams & Reservoirs

Pepacton Reservoir, on the East Branch of the Delaware, at twilight (left) and in the mists of dawn (below).

Photograph below by Scott Foster, New York City Department of Environmental Protection.

Indeed, the water of all this Catskill region is the best in the world. For the first few days, one feels as if he could almost live on the water alone; he cannot drink enough of it. In this particular it is indeed the good Bible land, "a land of brooks of water, of fountains and depths that spring out of valleys and hills."—JOHN BURROUGHS

The story of New York City's water is a tale of epic proportions illustrating that as a city grows, its citizens need to go progressively farther afield to get good water.

In the mid-1600s, when New Amsterdam was only a few thousand souls, the water came from shallow private wells. The first public well was dug at Bowling Green in 1677. It was another hundred years (1776) before the first reservoir, to collect water from wells, was built in lower Manhattan. The water was distributed through hollow logs laid under the streets. New York's population had grown by then to 22,000.

By 1830, a more extensive water system was in service, consisting of the downtown reservoir, a new one at Chambers Street, a fire tank at 13th Street, and a distribution grid of twelve-inch cast-iron pipes. As the city continued to grow, the well water became polluted and the supply inadequate, pushing the sources northward. Large cisterns were built to catch and store rainwater and springs were tapped at the upper end of Manhattan island.

Eventually, the island's need for water burst its bounds, and city fathers moved into what is today Westchester County to impound the water of the Croton River. The result, inaugurated in 1842, was an elaborate system made up of the Croton Reservoir; a classic, stone aqueduct modeled after Roman antecedents; and distribution reservoirs in Central Park below 86th Street and at 42nd Street (where the New York

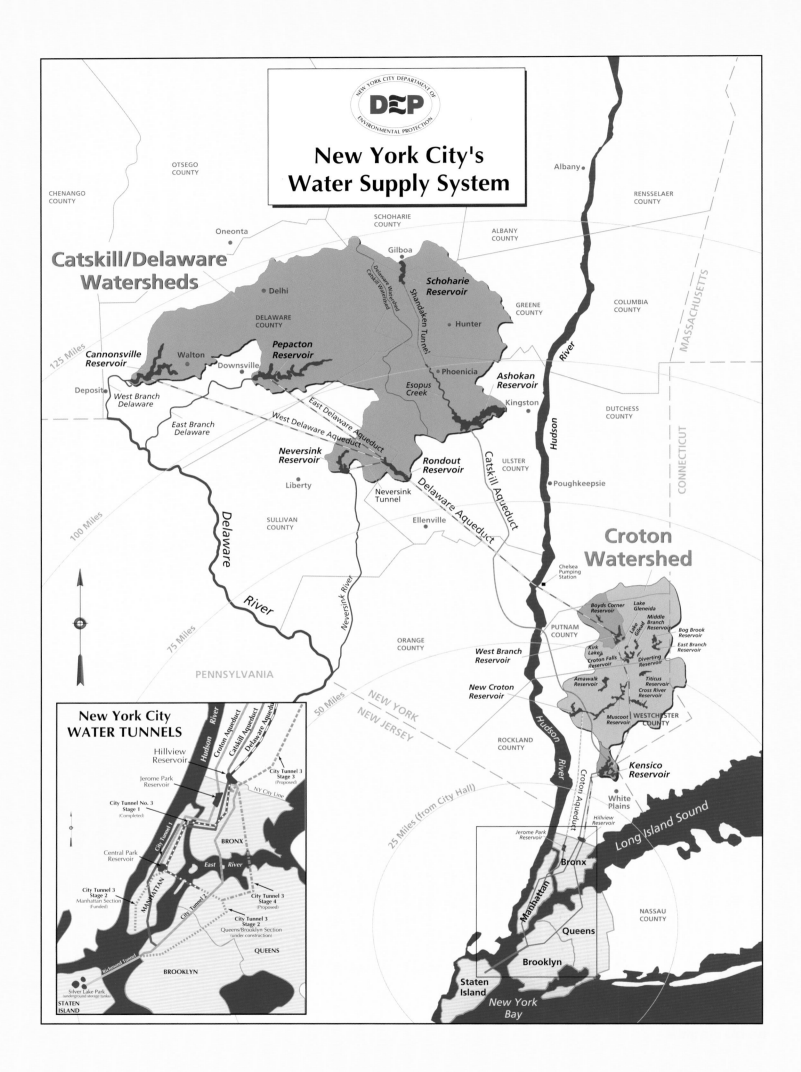

New York City's Water Supply System

Public Library now stands), capable of delivering 90 million gallons a day.

New reservoirs were added into the Croton system—Boyds Corner in 1873 and Middle Branch in 1878—and a second aqueduct placed in service in 1890. When the five boroughs were consolidated into New York City in 1898, so were their various water systems.

New York State got into the act in 1905, passing legislation that created the city's Board of Water Supply, which then launched a study leading to the decision to develop the Catskill region as an additional water source. First came the damming of Esopus Creek to create the Ashokan Reservoir in 1915, and over the ensuing fifty years, five more dams and their reservoirs were built: Schoharie (1926), Rondout (1950), Neversink (1953), Pepacton (1956), and Cannonsville (1967). Underground aqueducts were built connecting the Catskill region into the Croton system and so on down into the city. Today, the system includes eighteen reservoirs with a storage capacity of 550 billion gallons, delivering water to over 90 million people and more than a quarter-million industrial users. About 95 percent of the 1.5-billion-gallon-a-day consumption is delivered by gravity, with pumping during droughts and other times to maintain desired pressure.

Even with one of the world's largest concentrations of users, the New York metropolitan region's water supply remains practically unfiltered and is the envy of major cities everywhere. It has not been without pain and sacrifice, of course, that the system evolved. For example, soon after the Esopus and Schoharie dams came on line, squabbling began over sharing the water of the Delaware River.

Starting in 1925, the states of New York, Pennsylvania, and New Jersey tried to agree on the uses of the Delaware but failed. They tried and failed again in 1927. By 1931, mounting pressure from New York City for more water forced the issue into the United States Supreme Court, which declared: "A river is more than an amenity, it is a treasure. It offers a necessity of life that must be rationed among those who have power over it."

(Above) The Cannonsville dam looking downstream on October 10, 1963. Construction was nearly completed and the West Branch of the Delaware had been returned from a diversion channel at middle right to its old bed in the foreground.
Courtesy Board of Water Supply, City of New York.

(Left) Map of the New York City water system, showing the Catskill/Delaware and Croton watersheds with their connections to the city's water distribution network.
Courtesy New York City Department of Environmental Protection.

Neversink Reservoir, in March (left) and in early September (above).

Photograph at left by Scott Foster, New York City Department of Environmental Protection.

The court decreed that the city could divert 440 million gallons a day from the Delaware, but that a flow of 1,525 cubic feet per second had to be maintained past the gauging station at Montague, New Jersey. This came to be known as the "Montague formula" and was enforced by a federally appointed river master. The formula survived for twenty-three years until New York's growing water needs again forced a Supreme Court reckoning. The revised formula allowed an 800-mgd diversion provided that 1,750 cubic feet per second was maintained at Montague. By this time, the Neversink reservoir had been completed, and the plans were well underway for dams on both branches of the Delaware. With these three "holding tanks," a greater reserve would be available so that everyone's greater thirst could be slaked.

And many are the "thirsty." Industries want and get by far most of the Delaware's water. Over 85 percent of it goes to sustain the processes in shipyards, steel mills, oil refineries, chemical factories, and paper plants from Port Jervis down to Pea Patch Island off Delaware City. Farms at the upper end of the river, especially along the West Branch, need water for irrigation and livestock. Power companies on the Neversink and Mongaup rivers want water for their turbines. Cargo ships use it to ply the river as far north as Trenton. New Yorkers use

close to 1.5 billion gallons a day, most of it from the Delaware, to mix
with their Scotch and flush their toilets.

The forces of recreation had to wait until 1961 to be formally recognized as legitimate users of the Delaware's water. That was the year
President Kennedy and the governors of Delaware, New Jersey, New
York, and Pennsylvania signed the Delaware Basin Compact. It was a
"peace treaty" among all the water users, painfully hammered out over
the four to five years preceding its acceptance.

To reach this milestone, it took the catalytic force of two devastating
hurricanes in 1955, a $2 million congressional appropriation for consult-
ing reports, and the involvement of 19 federal agencies; 14 interstate
agencies; 43 state boards, departments, and commissions; and over
250 public and private water-using companies. Within the framework
of the Delaware Basin Compact all subsequent negotiations have taken
place, including those in the 1970s between the city and the state of New
York, which led to recreational releases from the Delaware watershed
reservoirs.

Of the six Catskill reservoirs built and maintained by New York City
for its water supply, all except the Schoharie have improved the trout
fishing above or below them, or both (albeit with the loss of more than
fifty-five miles of river fishing). The truth of this statement depends on

Ashokan Reservoir from High View (above) and Bear Kill Creek (right), feeder stream of Schoharie Reservoir.

Photographs by Scott Foster, New York City Department of Environmental Protection.

Cannonsville Reservoir in the fall (above) and Trout Creek (right), a tributary flowing into the Rondout Reservoir.

Photographs by Scott Foster, New York City Department of Environmental Protection.

the quality and continuity of the "recreational release" program, which is always subject to the threat of dry weather.

Gilboa Dam, which created Schoharie Reservoir when it was completed in 1925, releases modest amounts of water to the lower Schoharie, but there is very little trout fishing below the dam anyway. Whenever Schoharie Reservoir even approaches being full—and it fills quickly due to its small size—the city diverts its water through the Portal into Esopus Creek; this is done to the maximum allowed by law to keep from losing it downstream to the Mohawk, then the Hudson, and on out to sea.

And so our rivers roll on, punctuated here and there by dams, but flowing with the world's purest water. The tensions will always be present: along with the population, water needs will continue to grow, pitting urban consumers and officials against both the upcountry landowners, in whose backyards the rains fall, and the river fishermen, who can be counted on to oppose with tenacity any threat to the pristine homes of wild trout. As Sparse Grey Hackle once observed, "Of all the classic Catskill trout streams . . . only the Beaverkill and Willowemoc have not been dammed . . . the plans [to dam them] are not dead, just delayed. *'Vigilante!'*"

The Wulff Fishing School in session, viewed across one of the casting ponds.

TWENTY

Wulff Fishing School

I t was the vision of Lee Wulff when he passed seventy to settle in a prime, accessible fly-fishing location and open a fishing school with his wife, Joan, so that when he was gone, she would have a gainful, interesting life.

The location the Wulffs chose was the upper Beaverkill valley. The school opened in 1979 with courses that covered trout biology and behavior, artificial flies, streamcraft, tackle, and fly casting, the latter taking advantage of Joan's talents as a teacher and skills as former women's national or international casting champion for sixteen straight years. There was also an Atlantic salmon course based on Lee's knowledge and reputation as the world's leading angler for "the king of game fish."

When the Wulff school celebrated its twentieth anniversary recently, some two thousand students, from beginners to experts learning new tricks, had gone through its various courses. The Wulff Fishing School fills up each year mostly through word of mouth due to its unique

appeal among fly-fishing schools. There is, of course, the attraction of Joan Wulff, probably the best-known female fly fisher in the world; the long associations of its expert instructors, of which there is one for every four students; the teaching resources, which include the many books and films produced by Joan and Lee; the appeal of a private, family-run business with no commercial connections; and the pristine beauty of its 100-acre upper Beaverkill setting.

(Above) Joan and Lee Wulff outside their home, September 15, 1987.
Photograph by Ed Pfizenmaier.

(Left) In preparation for casting practice, Joan Wulff runs through the basics with her students.

(Right) Joan instructs the author in the double-haul with Lee's plane in the background.
Photograph by Ricker Winsor.

On April 28, 1991, in his eighty-sixth year, Lee Wulff climbed into his Piper Cub with a class in session, flew down the valley to Hancock to pick up a flight instructor in order to renew his pilot's license. They had completed the test and were returning to the field when Lee had a massive heart attack. The plane was too low for the instructor to keep it from crashing. He survived, but Lee did not.

The Wulff Fishing School, under Joan's direction, continues to build its reputation as one of the finest places to learn how to fly fish.

TWENTY-ONE

Literature of Catskill Fly Fishing

Consonant with its famous fly-fishing heritage, the Catskills has one of the richest literary traditions of any fly-fishing region. The photographed books in this chapter are from the libraries of Judith and James Bowman, the author, and the Anglers' Club of New York. I have given a brief comment on what a reader may look forward to in each of the listed titles.

Baker, R. Palmer, Jr. *The Sweet of the Year.* New York: William Morrow & Company, 1965. ✢ A conjuring of images at the reawakening of the valley and river in spring. "The great thing about trout fishing is that it makes the angler part of this young and lovely season," writes Baker.

Bergman, Ray. *Trout.* New York: Alfred A. Knopf, 1969. ✢ Many of Bergman's locations are Catskill streams, one of his favorites being the North Branch of Callicoon Creek. First published in 1938, his book is a perennial on the list of most beginning fly fishers; it was my first, given to me by my mother.

Bradley, William A. *Fly-Fishing Reminiscences of My Early Years at the Beaverkill Trout Club.* Pleasantville, N.Y.: Privately printed in an edition of 25 copies, 1929. ✢ Bradley printed and assembled this photo-album-style book for his fishing friends and dedicated it to "Lady Beaverkill," his beautiful, fly-fisher wife, who is turned out in what must be custom-cut waders.

Burke, Edgar. *American Dry Flies and How to Tie Them.* New York: Derrydale Press, 1930. ✢ At the request of Ed Hewitt, this 26-page book was illustrated by Dr. Burke with seven popular brown trout flies and published for the Anglers' Club to commemorate its 25th anniversary (1931). Copies were distributed to club members at the anniversary dinner. Burke also painted the fly patterns for early editions of Bergman's *Trout*.

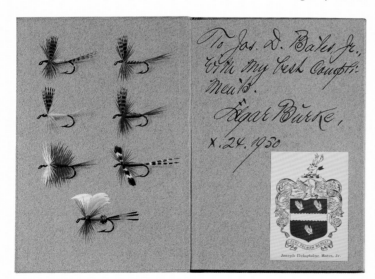

(Above) Edgar Burke, surgeon, artist, flytier, and angler, remarqued his book American Dry Flies and How to Tie Them *for Joe Bates, ". . . before breakfast this morning by artificial light, and hope the little paintings may somewhat enhance its value and that the volume will be a not unwelcome addition to your sporting library."*

(Left) The classics of the 1930s and 1940s, when book publishing was a genteel occupation and fly-fishing bookjacket illustrations conveyed the spirit of a gentlemanly pastime.

269

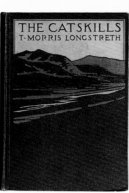

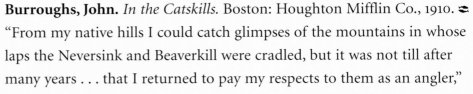

Burroughs, John. *In the Catskills.* Boston: Houghton Mifflin Co., 1910. ✜ "From my native hills I could catch glimpses of the mountains in whose laps the Neversink and Beaverkill were cradled, but it was not till after many years . . . that I returned to pay my respects to them as an angler," wrote Burroughs, the Catskill naturalist whose vivid essays gained him wide popularity as a goodhearted sage of nature.

Connett, Eugene V., III. *Any Luck?* New York: Windward House, 1933. ✜ Stories of the Neversink and other waters fished by Connett. One of angling's great bibliophiles, Connett founded the Derrydale Press, publisher of elegant sporting books, started the Anglers' Club *Bulletin*, and launched the Anglers' Club of New York library.

Cross, Reuben R. *Tying American Trout Lures.* New York: Dodd, Mead & Co., 1936. ✜ Cross's methods made him one of the best-known flytiers of his era. This book reveals his patterns and his techniques.
———. *Cowdung of Shin Crick.* New York: The Exposition Press, 1949. ✜ A rare little pamphlet written by Cross, with scatological exuberance, about a fictional country character "who won the love of all who lived in the rich river bottoms of Shin Crick."

Darbee, Harry. *The Compact Book of Fisherman's Tricks, Tips and Hints.* New York: J. Lowell Pratt & Co., 1967. ✜ Darbee's first book, illustrated by Francis W. Davis.

Darbee, Harry, with **Mac Francis.** *Catskill Flytier: My Life, Times, & Techniques.* Philadelphia: J.B. Lippincott, 1977. ✜ An intimate glimpse into the life of one of the Catskills' best-known flytiers, with practical advice on raising dun roosters, tying better flies, and fishing good.

Dimock, Anthony W. *Wall Street and the Wilds.* New York: Outing Publishing Co., 1915. ✜ The author, a successful stockbroker of the late 1800s, long had a dream to "live in the wilds." He finally found a valley in the Catskills "far removed from the fevered atmosphere of the Exchanges," where he fished and wrote "with the murmur of the stream in my ear."

Flick, Art. *New Streamside Guide to Naturals and Their Imitations.* New York: Crown Publishers, 1969. ✜ First published in 1947 and hailed as a "practical classic," Flick's book is a concise, authoritative work on naturals and their imitations. Begun when he helped Preston Jennings, Flick documented it with three more years' research on his home river, the

Schoharie. Color illustrations, with dressings, emergence tables, and sound advice on fishing the flies.

The Fly Fishers Club of Brooklyn 1895–1995. Portland, Maine: Ascensius Press, privately printed in an edition of 38 copies, 1997. ✷ The story of a club that defies change, so much so that all its lockers but one are reserved by dead members.

Foote, John Taintor. *Anglers All: The Great Fishing Stories of John Taintor Foote.* New York & London: D. Appleton-Century Co., 1947. ✷ Foote lived and fished in the Beaverkill valley when he wrote these enduring stories, including the George Baldwin Potter trilogy: "A Wedding Gift," "Fatal Gesture," and "Daughter of Delilah."

Francis, Austin McK. *Catskill Rivers: Birthplace of American Fly Fishing.* New York: Nick Lyons Books, 1983. ✷ Historical and physical portraits of the Beaverkill, Willowemoc, Neversink, Esopus, Schoharie, and Delaware—the rivers of Thaddeus Norris and Theodore Gordon, where American fly fishing came of age.

————, editor. *Sparse Grey Hackle.* New York: The Anglers' Club of New York, privately printed, 1993. ✷ Sparse was the chronicler of an angling era, particularly the golden age of Catskill fly fishing, that decade ending with 1940, when the place to be was at the camp of Edward R. Hewitt, home of the Neversink Rods.

Gerow, Joshua R. *Alder Lake: A Symposium of Nostalgic and Natural Observation.* Liberty, N.Y.: Fuelane Press, 1953. ✷ A lyrical recall of earlier days when Sam Coykendall owned this remote mountain lake that empties into the Beaverkill. Gerow: "Here in the stillness and fresh-ness of this tranquil retreat that creates its own environment, you will discover something more cognate and vitalic than in the affected cities and villages. Spirit of Alder, speak not to me of yesterday, for that is of the past; nor yet of today, for the lamps are lighted in the Lodge, but please, please whisper to me of the morrow."

Gill, Emlyn M. *Practical Dry-Fly Fishing.* New York: Charles Scribner's Sons, 1912. ✷ The first American book devoted to dry-fly fishing. Gill knew George LaBranche, whose book on the dry fly came out two years later; theories in both books were "field tested" at Ward's DeBruce Club Inn on the Willowemoc, where they often fished together.

Gingrich, Arnold. *The Well-Tempered Angler.* New York: Alfred A. Knopf, 1965. ✷ Plump with Catskill fish, fishing, and fishers, including Preston Jennings, Al McClane, Ed Hewitt, and others, illustrated with the free-flowing sketches of

John Groth, long-time art director of Gingrich's *Esquire* magazine.

———, editor. *American Trout Fishing: Theodore Gordon and a Company of Anglers.* New York: Alfred A. Knopf, 1966. ✍ Originally published in 1965 by the Theodore Gordon Flyfishers as *The Gordon Garland,* this book was renamed with the inclusion of an article by Gordon published only in England fifty years earlier. Several of its articles are about Catskill angling.

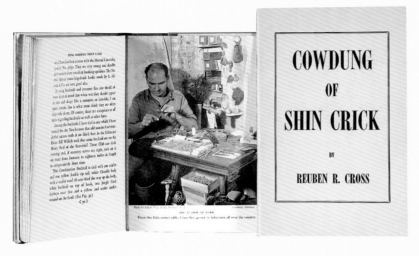

Hackle, Sparse Grey. *Fishless Days, Angling Nights.* New York: Crown Publishers, 1971. ✍ The trade edition of a 1954 privately published Anglers' Club volume. A collection of masterfully crafted, humorous stories, that for Harry Darbee was "the most entertaining fishing book I have ever read."

Hewitt, Edward R. *A Trout and Salmon Fisherman for Seventy-Five Years.* New York: Charles Scribner's Sons, 1950. ✍ Hewitt was a renaissance angler. An exacting fisherman, he took photos of artificials from under water, perfected stream management, originated the stonefly, skater, and bivisible, and pioneered as one of the first American nymph fishermen.

Holden, George Parker. *Streamcraft.* Cincinnati: Stewart and Kidd Co., 1920. ✍ The first book used by Harry Darbee as a text on flytying. Methods of Herman Christian, one of the earliest American dry-fly tiers.

Jennings, Preston J. *A Book of Trout Flies.* New York: Crown Publishers, 1970. ✍ Initially published by Derrydale Press in 1935, this book was the first reliable stream entomology to match the American hatch; it linked the most effective artificials with the naturals hatching at the moment. Jennings's research, mainly on the Esopus and other Catskill streams, enlisted the onstream observations of Roy Steenrod and Art Flick.

LaBranche, George M.L. *The Dry Fly and Fast Water.* New York: Charles Scribner's Sons, 1914. ✍ LaBranche's book eclipsed Gill's *Practical Dry-Fly Fishing* (1912) as "the American classic on dry-fly angling." The author emphasized precision casting, his forte, and urged his readers to rise through the ranks of angling development until they soon would be found "applying for the highest degree of the cult—'dry fly man.'"

Leiser, Eric. *The Dettes.* Fishkill, N.Y.: Willowkill Press, 1992. ✍ A devoted biography and family-album account of Walt, Winnie, and daughter

Mary Dette's sixty-year-and-counting contribution to the Catskill fly-tying tradition.

Longstreth, T. Morris. *The Catskills.* New York: The Century Co., 1918. ❧ Though Longstreth was only a sometime angler—he was mainly a hiker, canoer, and camper—his book is a beautifully original portrait of "America's first wilderness" that invites the reader to "follow up any brook only a little way, and you are certain to come upon mossy grottos, cool, damp, and very lonely, where you can have a waterfall to yourself."

Lyons, Nick. *The Seasonable Angler.* New York: Atlantic Monthly Press, 1970, 1999. ❧ Tales of the author's Catskill and other fishing. Nick's grandfather owned Kaaterskill Falls, near which as a lad of five he caught his first trout, leading to a life of fishing, publishing, and writing about fishing wherein he has become, said William W. Warner, "quite simply the tops, in stylish prose, gentle wit, and accumulated wisdom."

McDonald, John, editor. *The Complete Fly Fisherman: Notes and Letters of Theodore Gordon.* New York: Nick Lyons Books, 1989. ❧ The only personal records and observations of Theodore Gordon in book form, with a new introduction by McDonald. First published in 1947 by Scribners, this landmark work and the painstaking research behind it brought Gordon back into public view—after his articles and letters had lain forgotten for thirty years—solidly establishing him as "the father of modern American fly fishing."

———. *Quill Gordon.* New York: Alfred A. Knopf, 1972. ❧ This book merges all of McDonald's literary criticism on both Theodore Gordon and Dame Juliana Berners (from his *Origins of Angling).* Arnold Gingrich

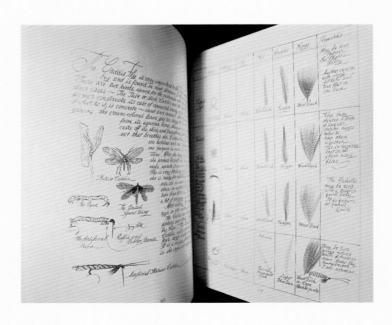

called the latter book "one of the most intense and perceptive feats of angling scholarship ever performed over the centuries in which fishing has been written about."

Norris, Thaddeus. *The American Angler's Book.* Philadelphia: E.H. Butler & Co., 1864. ❧ The first comprehensive work on American fly fishing, written by the best-known American angler of the nineteenth century. Wrote John McDonald, "He knew about everything there was to know in his time, put it all down in 1864, and thereby established the school of early American fly fishing with a rounded theory and practice."

Rhead, Louis. *American Trout-Stream Insects.* New York: Frederick A. Stokes Co., 1916. ❧ In his attempt at an angling entomology, Rhead failed to win the respect of his fellow anglers. His identification of stream insects, conducted on the Beaverkill, was overly casual, with a procession of "needletail duns, brown buzzes, nobby and fluffy spinners, little mauves, and gauze-wings," plus he tried to corner the dry-fly market by patenting his "Nature Lure" patterns, not giving their dressings in his book.

Salmon, Richard. *Trout Flies.* New York: Sportsman's Edge Press, 1975. ❧ It took twelve years to plan, illustrate, produce, and assemble what is more of an exhibition than a book—all the classic trout patterns arranged by columns of materials, each tipped onto the page, fulfilling Salmon's intent "to standardize, by color, texture, size, and name the stuff of which trout flies are made."

Van Put, Ed. *The Beaverkill.* New York: Lyons & Burford, 1996. ❧ A historical cornucopia on the Beaverkill river, its valley, and its fly-fishing heritage, drawn from the author's exhaustive ten-year delving into regional newspapers and periodicals.

White, Frederick. *The Spicklefisherman and Others.* New York: The Derrydale Press, 1928. ❧ Dedicated "To the Fishermen of the Beaverkill," where the author fished for 25 years, staying at Trout Valley Farm. The title character of his story is caught poaching a well-known trout club's water but manages to win over the stuffy member who wanted to throw him off.

Wright, Leonard M., Jr. *Fishing the Dry Fly as a Living Insect.* New York: E.P. Dutton, 1972. ❧ Wright gives his caddis-fly imitation plenty of action— "skittering" it across the surface instead of dead drift. He calls it an effective form of "heresy."

———. *Neversink: One Angler's Intense Exploration of a Trout River.* New York: Atlantic Monthly Press, 1991. ❧ A beautifully told, hands-on account of the river Len Wright has known intimately for over two decades: "I have drunk from it, fished it, studied it, and struggled to improve it."

"The end of a stiff fight."

Sparse Grey Hackle, chronicler of the golden era of Catskill angling, once observed to a fishing friend, "The Lord knows we can't fish, but at least we are literate."
Photograph by Larry Robins.

Index

THE 𝕰 BEAVERKILL PRESS

The text of this book has been set
in twelve-point Minion and printed
on 150g. GardaMatt Art by
Stamperia Valdonega, Verona, Italy

There are also 150 numbered
and signed deluxe copies,
in full-leather goatskin binding
and silk slipcase by
Legatoria Rigoldi, Milan, Italy.

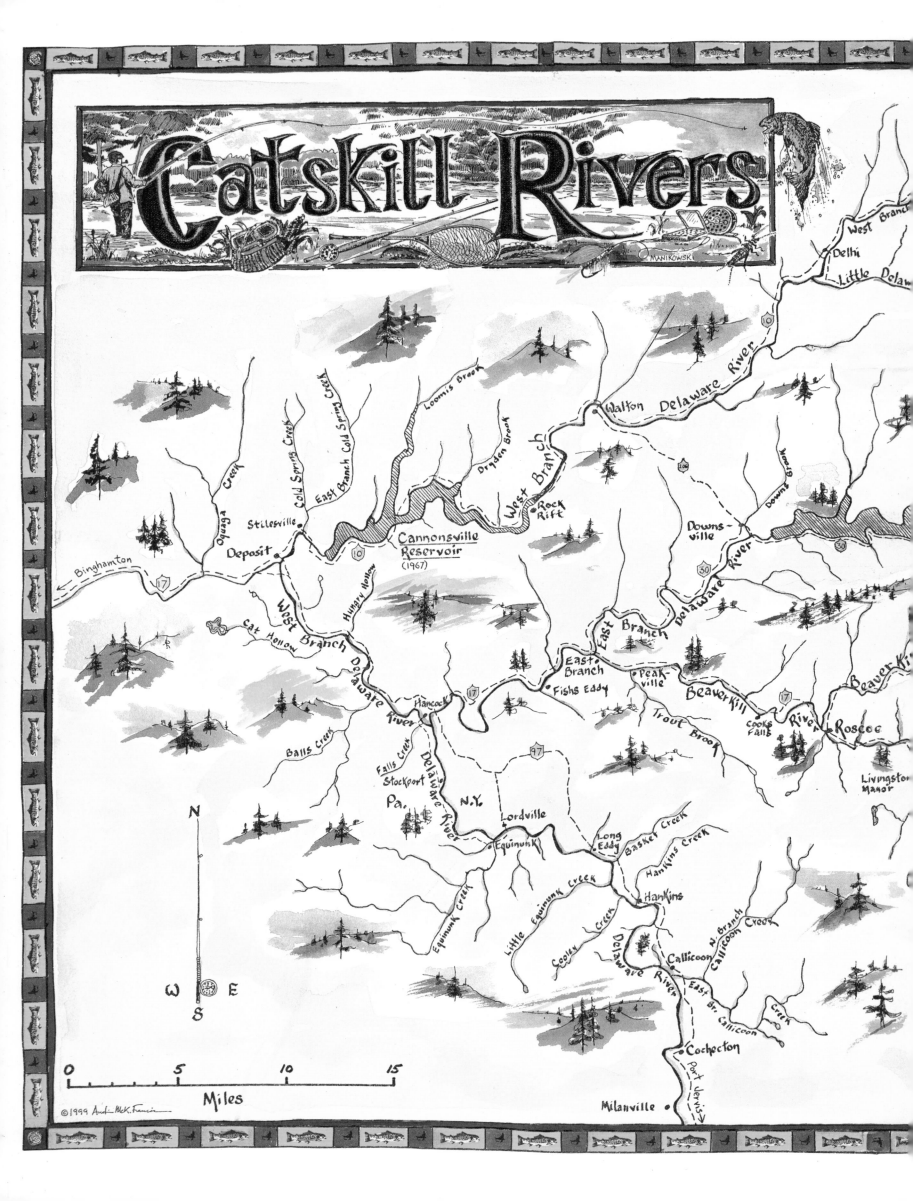